P9-DNX-736

QUICK TIPS
FOR
BUSY
FAMILIES

Also from Jay Payleitner

QUICK TIPS
FOR
BUSY
FAMILIES

SNEAKY STRATEGIES FOR RAISING GREAT KIDS

JAY PAYLEITNER

BETHANYHOUSE
a division of Baker Publishing Group
Minneapolis, Minnesota

© 2017 by Jay Payleitner

Published by Bethany House Publishers
11400 Hampshire Avenue South
Bloomington, Minnesota 55438
www.bethanyhouse.com

Bethany House Publishers is a division of
Baker Publishing Group, Grand Rapids, Michigan

ISBN 978-0-7642-1869-9

Printed in the United States of America

All rights reserved. No part of this publication may be reproduced, stored in a retrieval
system, or transmitted in any form or by any means—for example, electronic, photocopy,
recording—without the prior written permission of the publisher. The only exception is
brief quotations in printed reviews.

Library of Congress Cataloging-in-Publication Data is on file at the Library of Congress,
Washington, DC.

Scripture quotations, unless otherwise noted, are from the Holy Bible, New International
Version®. NIV®. Copyright © 1973, 1978, 1984, 2011 by Biblica, Inc.™ Used by permission
of Zondervan. All rights reserved worldwide. www.zondervan.com

Scripture quotations marked ESV are from The Holy Bible, English Standard Version®
(ESV®), copyright © 2001 by Crossway, a publishing ministry of Good News Publishers.
Used by permission. All rights reserved. ESV Text Edition: 2011

Scripture quotations marked NLT are from the Holy Bible, New Living Translation, copyright
© 1996, 2004, 2015 by Tyndale House Foundation. Used by permission of Tyndale House
Publishers, Inc., Carol Stream, Illinois 60188. All rights reserved.

Scripture quotations marked NKJV are from the New King James Version®. Copyright © 1982
by Thomas Nelson, Inc. Used by permission. All rights reserved.

Cover design by Darren Welch Design LLC

Author is represented by The Steve Laube Agency.

17   18   19   20   21   22   23   7   6   5   4   3   2   1

In keeping with biblical principles of
creation stewardship, Baker Publishing Group advocates the responsible
use of our natural resources. As a
member of the Green Press Initiative, our company uses recycled
paper when possible. The text paper
of this book is composed in part of
post-consumer waste.

This book is dedicated
to your kid's mom and dad

CONTENTS

Contents

Introduction

FYI. The following 144 quick tips for busy families are not so quick at all. You can certainly read each short chapter in a minute or two, but it may take a couple of decades before you realize the full benefit of some of these ideas.

That shouldn't be a surprise. As a parent, you know some rewards come sooner—a baby's smile or a valentine from a first grader. And some rewards will come later—a hug from a teenager or a thank-you from a new graduate. (Even later rewards include grandkids to spoil and the world-class retirement home your kids will choose for you someday.)

Not all of these tips are sneaky either. Some are gentle reminders of stuff you already know. Some are words and phrases you can speak into the lives of your kids. Some of these tips might be considered "parenting hacks." Some are spiritual truths critical for every member of your family. And some are semi-brilliant revelations I learned in the process of raising five successful kids who still get along and still enjoy hanging out with their mom and dad.

You will also discover boundaries to set, memories to make, and life lessons to cram into their tiny skulls. Along the way, I reveal some personal parenting fails and satisfying wins. Hey, no one's perfect.

The chapters are in no particular order. We'll share a laugh at one page. And we'll get real serious a few pages later. You are invited to read the entire book in one sitting or one chapter at a time. If you're a blogger, teacher, or small-group leader, you have permission to repurpose a reasonable number of these ideas as long as you give credit where credit is due.

As always, I love to hear any input from moms and dads who may have their own parenting tips or a fresh spin on something they found in one of my books. Track me down at jaypayleitner.com.

Realize Every Kid Is Different

K ids don't come with the word *musician, athlete, scholar, entrepreneur,* or *artist* stamped on their forehead. Rita and I have four sons, one daughter, four daughters-in-law, and six young grandkids. All with different gifts and personalities.

Raising our family, we assumed our five kids with the same genetic makeup would follow five similar paths. But during their formative years, we seemed to have three natural musicians, two artists, three voracious readers, two math whizzes, two techies, three writers, one scientist, three strategic thinkers, two dreamers, and five athletes. Even now, as life unfolds, we see a continuing evolution of passions and personalities.

Trust me, it's a mistake to slap a label on a kid and put them in a box.

On the other hand, part of our job as parents is to help our children head in the direction consistent with their God-given gifts and passions. Sometimes that means nudging them back on track. Sometimes it means watching uneasily as their plans naturally derail. Sometimes all we have to do is stand back and applaud.

The key might be to encourage young people to throw themselves 110 percent into life. When their best efforts come up short, then they'll know to move on to another life pursuit. In other words, encourage exploration and discourage a slacker mentality.

Take heart. The next 143 chapters offer an array of invaluable, unexpected, comforting, quizzical, and sneaky strategies for helping your kids meet their full potential.

You may be called to enter their world. Or invite them to enter your world. You may be given an assignment to implement right away. You may read some strategy that seems insignificant and then suddenly it comes in handy in the not-so-distant future.

You will be reminded that the same child may need to be hugged or disciplined or rescued all in the same twenty-four-hour period. You will be challenged to be their best teacher and biggest cheerleader. Some chapters suggest things you need to give your kids: boundaries, compliments, chores, memories, secrets to success, and real-life lessons you learned the hard way.

Combined, these chapters are designed to celebrate and connect families, and help you bring out the best in each other.

Isn't that what you want? Every kid is different. But each one should be given every chance to live God's best plan for their best life.

Candy Land Penance

One of my wife's brilliant punishments for our boys was thirty minutes of hard labor. Specifically, one game of Candy Land with their little sister. If you've got older kids and younger kids, that's an idea worth the price of this book. Everyone wins. The younger sib gets to spend quality time with the cool, typically too-busy older sib. The older sib suffers a not-too-painful consequence for a minor offense. You get thirty minutes of peace and quiet. It's foolproof, unless . . .

Alec—thirteen years older than Rae Anne—devised a work-around. Before the game started, he stacked the Candy Land deck of cards. Rae Anne's first pick was Queen Frostine, followed by double purple, followed by another double purple, followed by a blue. Game over. Rae Anne was ecstatic with her easy victory. Alec was out of the doghouse in less than five minutes. All of which left Mom wondering if Alec should be rewarded or re-punished.

Rita decided it was all good. Until . . . the next time, when Alec stacked the deck again. But this time, he arranged the cards so *he* won in four moves, while his little sister drew red, purple, yellow, blue, which meant she crawled ahead one tiny space each turn while he leapfrogged across the finish line. Rae Anne was not happy. Alec was quite amused. And Rita couldn't help but laugh.

Next time, it got even worse. (Or better.) Alec spent a little extra time stacking the deck. This time, Rae Anne jumped out to the lead, quickly got one space from the finish line, then on the next card, she was sent all the way back to the Peppermint Forest, where she dawdled for several cards, then sprinted ahead only to be ripped back to the plums, molasses, or whatever candy swamp was on the board back then. Alec "somehow" pulled victory from the jaws of defeat. It was a classic case of an older brother torturing a younger sister. It was also the last time we used Candy Land as punishment.

Still, Candy Land penance is highly recommended. That is, until your older child figures out the option of card stacking and sibling torture. Which isn't really so bad. You will at least get a good family story to tell for years to come.

Six Games for Road Trips

A series of grueling car trips should be a requirement for graduating childhood. Hours of transportational incarceration belted onto vinyl seats in a confined space with limited airflow fosters critical lessons in patience, endurance, self-discipline, and dealing with combative siblings. This current generation of whiny passengers, with their portable screens, headphones, smartphones, gaming devices, and unlimited entertainment selections, don't know how good they have it.

I'm inclined to believe plugged-in kids are missing out. The most obvious example? Their electronic devices are keeping them from experiencing the great long-haul tradition of road trip games. Consider these classic games that can only be played by staring out of car windows.

License Plate Search—Of course, the goal is to find one from every state—as a competition between individuals or as a unified team. Award bonus points for farthest state, Canadian provinces, and government plates. Spotting a car from Alaska or Hawaii earns triple points.

The Alphabet Game—Find words on billboards, highway signs, and bumper stickers that begin with letters *A* through *Z*. It's actually quite painful to pass a *Q* when you're still looking for a *P*.

Slug Bug (aka Punch Buggy)—This game doesn't work anymore. There simply aren't enough Volkswagen Beetles on the road. With this book, let's begin a new game called "Camper Hammer" or "Ragtop Bop" anytime you pass an RV or a convertible. Try it out and let me know how it goes. Same rules as Slug Bug: Give a shout-out every time you see one and playfully punch someone.

Counting Cows—Each kid or team gets all the cows on their side of the car. If you pass a herd, count fast and be honest. If you pass a cemetery on your side, your cattle count goes back to zero. Each round ends when the driver puts the car into park for any reason.

Count Anything—Water towers, red barns, animal carcasses, windmills, motorcycles, cars with stuff on their roof racks, cop cars, church steeples, or anything! Have everyone in the car (except the driver) pick an item and see who wins. Hint: If you get off the expressway, unusual items like wishing wells, blue tarps, garden gnomes, and shiny garden spheres really start to add up. (It's truly surprising how many blue tarps are visible from the road.)

Car Color Challenge—Each kid chooses a color. First to reach twenty items wins. Hint for Mom or Dad: Silver always wins. So make sure the youngest child takes silver!

Odometer Math—There are quite a few games you can play with your instrument panel. Have your crew guess how many telephone poles are in a mile. Point to a distant water tower, overpass, or other object on the skyline and have your passengers guess how far away it is.

There are all kinds of other games you might play in the car, such as Twenty Questions, I Spy, and Fortunately/Unfortunately. But the above games can only be played in a moving vehicle. That's why, even if you have the budget to fly, you need occasionally to pile the crew into the SUV or minivan and hit the road.

$ **15** off

your next $75 purchase
Limit one coupon per transaction.

Valid through 10/07/2017

470001556193432

$ **15** off

your next $75 purchase
Limit one coupon per transaction.

Valid 10/14/2017 - 10/28/2017

470001556193494

$ **15** off

your next $75 purchase
Limit one coupon per transaction.

Valid 10/21/2017 - 11/18/2017

470001556193555

This one-time use promotional card ("Card") is good for $15 off any in-stock or special order merchandise single receipt purchase of $75 or more (calculated before taxes & after applicable discounts). Card is not a credit or debit card, has no implied warranties & can't be used in conjunction with any other coupon/discount (including, but not limited to, 5% Lowe's consumer credit discount; Lowe's military discount; Lowe's employee discounts; Lowe's Price Match Guarantee; contractor packs; manager discretion price adjustments; Lowe's volume discount programs such as Quote Support Program "QSP"; government contract pricing; or any other special pricing/discount programs). Card is not redeemable for cash, not transferable & can't be replaced if lost or stolen. Void if altered, defaced, copied, transferred, or sold through any on-line auction or otherwise. Limit 1 Card per household. Redeemable in-store, on Lowes.com, and Lowe's mobile applications. Not valid on: LowesforPros.com; previous sales; multiple transactions; purchase of services, installation, or extended protection plans; gift cards; Weber products; Dacor, ICON, Fisher & Paykel, Monogram, Smeg, or Liebherr brand appliances (some brands not available in all markets/stores); or clearance appliances. Customer must pay applicable sales tax. Card can't be used to make payments on any charge or credit account. Cash Value: 1/100 cent. Valid in the U.S. only & expires on the date listed. Lowe's reserves the right to withdraw the Card at any time for any reason.

©2017 Lowe's. LOWE'S and Gable Mansard Design are registered trademarks of LF, LLC

This one-time use promotional card ("Card") is good for $15 off any in-stock or special order merchandise single receipt purchase of $75 or more (calculated before taxes & after applicable discounts). Card is not a credit or debit card, has no implied warranties & can't be used in conjunction with any other coupon/discount (including, but not limited to, 5% Lowe's consumer credit discount; Lowe's military discount; Lowe's employee discounts; Lowe's Price Match Guarantee; contractor packs; manager discretion price adjustments; Lowe's volume discount programs such as Quote Support Program "QSP"; government contract pricing; or any other special pricing/discount programs). Card is not redeemable for cash, not transferable & can't be replaced if lost or stolen. Void if altered, defaced, copied, transferred, or sold through any on-line auction or otherwise. Limit 1 Card per household. Redeemable in-store, on Lowes.com, and Lowe's mobile applications. Not valid on: LowesforPros.com; previous sales; multiple transactions; purchase of services, installation, or extended protection plans; gift cards; Weber products; Dacor, ICON, Fisher & Paykel, Monogram, Smeg, or Liebherr brand appliances (some brands not available in all markets/stores); or clearance appliances. Customer must pay applicable sales tax. Card can't be used to make payments on any charge or credit account. Cash Value: 1/100 cent. Valid in the U.S. only & expires on the date listed. Lowe's reserves the right to withdraw the Card at any time for any reason.

©2017 Lowe's. LOWE'S and Gable Mansard Design are registered trademarks of LF, LLC

This one-time use promotional card ("Card") is good for $15 off any in-stock or special order merchandise single receipt purchase of $75 or more (calculated before taxes & after applicable discounts). Card is not a credit or debit card, has no implied warranties & can't be used in conjunction with any other coupon/discount (including, but not limited to, 5% Lowe's consumer credit discount; Lowe's military discount; Lowe's employee discounts; Lowe's Price Match Guarantee; contractor packs; manager discretion price adjustments; Lowe's volume discount programs such as Quote Support Program "QSP"; government contract pricing; or any other special pricing/discount programs). Card is not redeemable for cash, not transferable & can't be replaced if lost or stolen. Void if altered, defaced, copied, transferred, or sold through any on-line auction or otherwise. Limit 1 Card per household. Redeemable in-store, on Lowes.com, and Lowe's mobile applications. Not valid on: LowesforPros.com; previous sales; multiple transactions; purchase of services, installation, or extended protection plans; gift cards; Weber products; Dacor, ICON, Fisher & Paykel, Monogram, Smeg, or Liebherr brand appliances (some brands not available in all markets/stores); or clearance appliances. Customer must pay applicable sales tax. Card can't be used to make payments on any charge or credit account. Cash Value: 1/100 cent. Valid in the U.S. only & expires on the date listed. Lowe's reserves the right to withdraw the Card at any time for any reason.

©2017 Lowe's. LOWE'S and Gable Mansard Design are registered trademarks of LF, L

Don't Hide Your Yearbook

Your initial instinct may be to hide your high school yearbook from your kids. For three reasons.

One, the pictures are horrid or embarrassing or both. That hair. That bow tie. That neckline. What were you thinking?

Two, the scribbled memories of your classmates may reveal that you didn't always make the best decisions during your formative years. Things like "I'll always remember that weekend at Corman's cottage," "Rocky Mountain High," "Prom Night 2004 XXXOOO!!!" or "PTYP FOREVER." When your kids read those decades-old scribbles, you may have some serious explaining to do.

Three, your own actual academic achievements and involvement in clubs, sports, and other extracurricular activities may not match the expectations you've presented to your offspring. After all, how can you justify pushing your kids to be more involved, when you were a total slacker in high school?

Well, that was then. This is now. During this season of life, your yearbook is a fabulous tool for getting your kids to talk about their hopes and dreams, fears and failures, habits and hang-ups. It's really okay for parents to admit they made mistakes or have regrets. It's healthy for kids to imagine Mom and Dad when they were in middle school or high school.

Accidentally leave your yearbook on the kitchen table and get ready for some hearty laughs and heartfelt conversations with your kids.

5

Blasting Classical Music

Rita had this silly idea that classical music might be soothing to a crying baby or fussy toddler. So she set the far-right FM-radio push button in our minivan to 98.7 WFMT, Chicago's legendary classical music station. Her idea didn't work, but the push button remained set.

A few years later, it did work. Sort of.

When our school-age kids would start acting up or playing one of their favorite torture games like "Not touching, can't get mad," she would punch the far-right button. Then crank the volume. The loud strings and orchestrations weren't necessarily soothing, but it was a signal.

The kids knew when they heard WFMT it was their last chance to behave before Rita would pull over the minivan and lay down the law. The signal worked because we almost never listened to Vivaldi or Chopin in our house, so the music stood out as different.

I suppose blasting polka, rap, or bagpipes might also have done the job. But classical music worked nicely for Rita because it's not so painful to endure. It was just out of the ordinary.

The real benefit here is that Rita never had to scream, "Cut it out back there!" from the driver's seat. Classical music did that instead. To this day, I don't know if this parenting hack left any permanent anti-Beethoven bias with any of our kids. Maybe.

Honor Apologies

Believe it or not, when kids mess up, they know it. They have instant regrets. In most cases, they would love to be able to make things right ASAP. But it's not easy to apologize. It can be very hard to confess to Mom and Dad. It shouldn't be, but all kinds of emotions, egos, and fears get in the way.

They think you're going to be mad. They are frustrated with themselves. They don't know what kind of punishment might be waiting for them. If their guilt and shame fester for a while, they may even start to believe they are not worthy of your love. Consider the thought process of the Prodigal Son when he found himself broke, lonely, and yearning for the pigs' food.

> When he came to his senses, he said, "How many of my father's hired servants have food to spare, and here I am starving to death! I will set out and go back to my father and say to him: Father, I have sinned against heaven and against you. I am no longer worthy to be called your son; make me like one of your hired servants."
>
> Luke 15:17–19

As you may recall, the father was regularly scanning the horizon, praying for the safe return of his rebellious son. There was no malice in that father's heart. Only love. But the son didn't know that.

> So he got up and went to his father. But while he was still a long way off, his father saw him and was filled with compassion for him; he ran to his son, threw his arms around him and kissed him. The son said to him, "Father, I

have sinned against heaven and against you. I am no longer worthy to be called your son."

But the father said to his servants, "Quick! Bring the best robe and put it on him. Put a ring on his finger and sandals on his feet. Bring the fattened calf and kill it. Let's have a feast and celebrate. For this son of mine was dead and is alive again; he was lost and is found." So they began to celebrate.

Luke 15:20–24

Most readers of the story of the Prodigal Son think of it as a lesson for those who are lost, hungry, and seeking redemption. Well, that's only part of the story. For parents, the lesson might be "When a wayward son or daughter—or even a small child who makes a small mistake—comes to you with sincere regrets, run to them. Eagerly accept your child's apology. Sweep that prodigal into your arms. And maybe even throw a little a party."

Stash Markers and Poster Boards

You cannot rescue your kids from every crisis. As a matter of fact, you don't want to. Sometimes they need to suffer the consequences of procrastination and forgetfulness. That's really the only way they will ever learn to plan ahead and meet deadlines.

But once in a while, it's wonderfully satisfying to play the role of hero. This sneaky plan makes it remarkably easy for you to earn hero status. Next time you're at Walmart, Hobby Lobby, or a discount office supply store, spend about twenty bucks on a nice set of colored markers and a half dozen assorted poster boards. Then hide them. Behind a sofa. Under a bed. In a back closet. And forget about them.

Sometime in the next year or so, your son or daughter is going to come to you as bedtime approaches with a slight look of terror on their little face. "I need to make a poster that's due tomorrow." Maybe it's for a last-minute student political campaign. Maybe it's a visual aid to support a speech they wrote a week ago. Maybe it's one of those fun, easy projects that got set aside because the young scholar had been concentrating efforts on more difficult assignments. In any case, they know they blew it. They know it's late. And they know you are their only hope.

You could say, "Too bad, so sad. Hope you learned your lesson." You could race to the twenty-four-hour drugstore across town and pay triple for some bent white cardboard and boring markers. Or you could magically produce the exact-right supplies from your hidden stash.

Your child will be amazed and grateful. Frankly, you'll feel pretty good about the way things worked out as well. Nice job, heroic parent of the year!

PEZ Dispenser Magic

Give a kid a PEZ candy dispenser and, with few exceptions, joy enters the room. Why? To begin with, it's unexpected. A child opens a sad-looking brown bag at the cafeteria lunch table or slumps into the kitchen after a tough day in fourth grade, and then bam! Suddenly they are in possession of a beloved cartoon character with a plastic head on a plastic stand filled with candy! It's simply too good to be true.

Plus, it's not an expensive gift, so the child doesn't need to write a thank-you note or feel indebted to the PEZ giver. And golly gee whillikers, the candy is sharable! One for you. Two for me.

Best of all, PEZ dispenser magic works on adults too. You may even want to have a secret stash of assorted PEZ dispensers for use anytime and anywhere.

Twenty-one Things to Write on a Sticky Note

Since their official introduction in 1980, Post-it Notes have become ubiquitous purveyors of critical or not-so-critical information in offices, schools, and homes around the world, as well as the bestselling product of 3M. But I think the best use of those little yellow squares might be for parents to jot love notes to their kids.

Let's quickly consider twenty-one messages you might leave on a mirror, lunch box, book bag, cereal box, bike handlebar, bedroom door, shower door, piano, clarinet, alarm clock, refrigerator, stuffed animal, or Bible.

"Have a great day!" "Nice job." "Proud of you." "XXXO" "Be epic today!" "Good luck on your geography test!" "Spaghetti tonight!" "Happy half-birthday." "Off to NYC until Thursday. I'll miss you. Love, Mom." "Good morning, Beautiful!" "Study hard!" ":)" "Will you play me a song tonight?" "Looking forward to our date tonight! Love, Dad." "Missed you last night!" "Sorry about our argument. Love, Dad." "This bathroom is a mess. But you're still the best." "Thanks for being you." "Love you." "Read Isaiah 41:10." "Romans 8:28."

Of course, phrases like these can be vocalized to your kids as they head out the door. You can also whisper them as you kiss their forehead after bedtime prayers. But there's something special about seeing the words written down. Leaving sticky notes is especially valuable when busy parents and busy kids seem to be racing past each other for several days in a row.

Mom and Dad, don't be surprised if your son or daughter keeps those Post-it Notes stuck where you stick them. Or maybe they'll peel them off and keep them forever in a journal or treasure box.

Take Two-Person Photos

My latest family photo—me, my bride, our five kids, four daughters-in-law, and four grandkids—has sixteen people in it. Rita and me. Alec and Lindsay. Randall, Rachel, Judah, and Gideon. Max, Megan, Jack, and Reese. Isaac, Kaitlin, and Emerson. And our final college student, Rae Anne. Note: Kaitlin is expecting. And we'll see how God continues to bless us!

The times when we all get together are precious. We try to take a group shot to document the moment forever. Those pics make it into often-liked Instagram posts, Facebook cover photos, and PowerPoint presentations.

But we have a group of photos that are even more precious. It's the two-fers. Those are single pics that happened to catch two members of the family in a moment of joy or adventure. We have several of them, nicely framed on a special shelf in our hallway. Randy, waist-high in the Atlantic Ocean, with Rae Anne standing on his shoulders. Three-year-old Isaac listening to Max's tummy with one of those yellow-and-blue Fisher-Price stethoscopes. Newborn Alec and me on the day I became a father. And, of course, Rita nuzzling one of her grandbabies. (You can see what I mean on my website: jaypayleitner.com.)

This is not a breakthrough idea, but it is worth mentioning. Especially if you have a bigger family. Two-person photos become a connecting point for those two individuals. Whether it's a toddler and a great grandmother, cousins who happen to be the same age, or a teenager goofing off with their much younger sibling. Don't be surprised when those photos become favorite posts acknowledging milestones over social media.

Yes, take group shots. And solo shots. But never hesitate to hold up your camera or smartphone and say, "Hey, you two! Pretend like you like each other."

Buy Them One Thing

Y ou will find great satisfaction in this parenting strategy because now you can watch someone else's child throw a major tantrum at the local supermarket while knowing you will never again have to endure that personal parenting nightmare. With sincere empathy and great relief, this strategy will enable you to walk right past an ill-mannered brat rolling on the tile floor of aisle six while your perfect child sits calmly in the shopping cart. Even though you have every right, you probably should refrain from murmuring, "Tsk, tsk, tsk." Instead, nod with soulful compassion because you've been there.

It's a three-part plan. First, establish grocery shopping as an adventure and a privilege. *"We get to go shopping today! Won't that be fun!? You and Mommy are going to find lots of good things to eat, and stuff for cleaning, and food for Fido!"*

Second, offer even more good news: *"You get to choose one thing from the store all for yourself! What will you choose?"* Following through on that promise, your child, within reason, gets just about anything she requests. That may include Cocoa Puffs, ice cream, dog biscuits for Fido, or even a potted daffodil for the neighbor.

Third—and this is key—if your child asks for something else, be surprised, and absolutely firm. "You've already chosen your one thing!" If she fusses, leave the store. Even if the cart is full of groceries. Even if you need those groceries for dinner tonight. Your young shopping assistant needs to know that fussing and pouting is not allowed in stores.

P.S. On the way out, you should probably let a store employee know, with your apologies, that you won't be back and the cart has some things that need to be refrigerated or frozen.

Celebrate Moments of Maturity

Just when you think your nine-year-old is a total lost cause, that sneaky little darling will do something that blows you away. Something that says, "I'm growing up and taking responsibility for my actions." Or even more amazing, "The world doesn't revolve around me."

What might be some examples of this new miraculous behavior? They clean up the cat vomit without being told. They finish their homework before turning on the gaming console. They replace the empty roll of toilet paper. They return the family tape dispenser or stapler to its proper cubby. At Dairy Queen, they order a Dilly bar or small cone instead of an extra large Blizzard. They initiate a meaningful conversation with a teacher, coach, neighbor, or pastor. They volunteer out of the blue to help with the dishes, the trash, the dusting, the raking, the laundry, or the baby.

Later, ask them over to your desk or quiet corner and open your Bible to 1 Corinthians 13:11 NLT: "When I was a child, I spoke and thought and reasoned as a child. But when I grew up, I put away childish things." Without too much fanfare, tell your child you noticed. You noticed how they're growing up and voluntarily taking on new responsibilities. Tell them how awesome they are. Let them know you look forward to seeing how God will use them in the years to come.

Then joke with them about not growing up too quickly: "In the next few years, your life is going to get jam-packed with all kinds of new and amazing opportunities. I'll miss my little girl (little guy). But I'm looking forward to the next season of your life. I will always be here for you."

The Library Card Initiation

D on't sign up your three-year-old for a library card. Your son or daughter won't fully appreciate the significance and won't remember the moment.

Instead, wait until your children can sign their name, pick out their own books, and be responsible for their safe return. Books are precious things. The very fact that a giant brick building (and staff) would trust you with its most valuable possessions is a privilege not to be taken for granted.

Make your child's first library card an initiation into a new world of knowledge and discovery. This occasion is also the perfect time to teach some critical life skills. That includes library etiquette, such as never ever running and reduced vocal volumes. (Don't you miss those days when librarians actually shushed anyone who did not whisper?) Dutifully describe the Dewey Decimal System. Let them try the digital card catalog. Walking the stacks is a humbling experience. Reserving a book that's currently checked out teaches patience and somehow connects you with all the other library patrons.

Most important, just spending time in your local library exposes your children to the amazing and eye-opening world of ideas that falls between all those book covers.

If It's Important to Your Kids, It's Important to You

When he was in middle school, my oldest son, Alec, had collected more than a hundred Orel Hershiser baseball cards and wore a Dodgers baseball cap everywhere he went. For that season of life, it became part of his identity.

On a cross-country family vacation, he accidentally left that beat-up blue cap at a greasy-spoon diner we had stopped at for breakfast. By the time Alec realized it, we had traveled some thirty miles. I knew we had dozens of ball caps at home. But I also knew that one particular cap was more than a typical ball cap. I wasn't happy about it, but I made an illegal U-turn on the expressway and drove back to retrieve it.

That cap was important to Alec, so as a committed parent, it was important to me.

Dad Tucks In

Statistically, moms spend more time with kids than dads. To counter that inequity, let's just make a rule. Whenever possible, dad tucks in. The benefits are many. Mom gets a break. Dad gets a clear assignment that he can check off his to-do list. The kids get a daily chance to spend time one-on-one with that shadowy figure who otherwise might only get acknowledged on weekends.

In the early years, the commitment is minimal. In six minutes, you page through a picture book, share one event of the day, say a prayer, kiss them good-night, and whisper, "Sweet dreams." As they get older, you'll want to carve out a bit more time. Questions, conversations, and prayer topics will become more in-depth. That's a good thing. You want to know what's on their hearts and minds. Don't be surprised if your curious kids bring up topics that trigger some fresh ideas you haven't considered for years. Or ever.

Perhaps the greatest benefit of tucking in is the chance to put the cares and concerns of the day into proper perspective. Share a bit about your own day. Listen to their highs and lows. Nod and empathize. Celebrate small victories. Never minimize their concerns, fears, or grief. Occasionally, look for opportunities to sneak in biblical truths. Try saying things like "It'll be interesting to see how God uses that experience down the road," "You know what? You may have uncovered one of your spiritual gifts today," or "We need to make plans, but sometimes God guides us down a path we never anticipated."

In the stillness of their bedroom, your time together should set the stage for restful sleep and hope-filled dreams. Keep praying and kissing them good-night—even through the teen years. (Especially through the teen years!) When they finally head off on their own—college, the military, marriage, career—you will miss that time together. I promise: they will too.

Looking way down the road, I also promise you will find great satisfaction when you realize that your kids are tucking in their own kids.

Worth noting: In your home, if Dad generally spends more time with the kids . . . Mom tucks in.

Plan to Flex

ost books by parenting authorities extol the virtues of organizing and planning. Even this book suggests that doing certain procedures certain ways will result in some kind of guaranteed results. Hogwash.

Absolutely, there's a place for job charts, schedules, and calendars. Homework needs to get done. Meetings need to meet. A little structure makes life so much more pleasant. You certainly don't want to be that family who always arrives late, doesn't follow through on commitments, and shows no respect for the time and efforts of others.

But there has to be room for the occasional minor crisis, rabbit trail, or better opportunity that may come along. Sure, you promised to be at a certain place at a certain time prepared with certain supplies to achieve a certain goal. But that won't always happen. The little one's diaper explodes. A neighbor has an emergency. The office supply store has run out of purple foam core. Without warning, seven other items appear on your must-do list that happen to be more important than your original goal. Plus, it's a hot summer day and Dairy Queen has two-for-one Blizzards.

For better or worse, your previously precious plan has been preempted, proving once again, there are few guarantees on this side of heaven. But you knew that. You knew that patience and humility were just as important as achievement and personal glory. Which is why you continue to make plans, but hold them loosely. You and your family are living, breathing proof of the truth found in Proverbs 16:9 NLT: "We can make our plans, but the Lord determines our steps."

Throw Paper or Rock Accordingly

Hundreds of hours of undocumented fake research have concluded that the initial throw for any child between the ages of four and nine playing Rock-Paper-Scissors will be *Scissors*. Go ahead, try it.

This information comes in remarkably handy on two occasions. One is when a youngster needs an emotional boost for whatever reason. Simply challenge them to a quick game and throw *Paper*. When they win, react with just enough distress. *"You rascal. You scoundrel. Oh, fine. You won. I'll get you next time."*

The inside information is also quite valuable when a child needs to be put in his place. *"Hey, champ! Rock-Paper-Scissors. You and me. Right here, right now. Loser takes out the trash. Ready?"* Then you throw *Rock*, thereby earning the right to crush their *Scissors*. When they say, "Two out of three," make sure to deny their request because victory on your next throw down is no longer assured.

Like so many other parenting hacks, use this one sparingly. Your sharp third grader will very likely catch on.

Keep the GPS Option Open

There's a lot of baggage that comes with modern technology. Our kids are always three clicks away from an overdose of crud, misinformation, and time wasters. You already know the frustration that comes from having your entire family in one location while every single nose is eight inches from a tiny screen.

But there's some good stuff too. Apps and websites like Tumblr, Instagram, and Vine give you previously unavailable insight into the lives of your kids and their friends. Phones keep you in touch and leave no excuses for lack of communication. If you stay mostly nonjudgmental, your kids may even share their selfies, pins, profiles, and other data.

There's also another parenting tech option that you'll want to keep handy in your parenting toolbox. Specifically, that's tracking your kids via GPS on their phones. I can already hear your kids screaming, "No!"

For the most part, I agree with them. In a few years, when your sixteen-year-old daughter is out with friends, she certainly doesn't want to feel the pressure of twenty-four-hour surveillance. Indeed, most parents don't want to be tracking their child's every move. *"Honey, Brianna just left the O'Malley's and she's headed down Park Street at thirty-six miles per hour, and it looks like she may be stopping at Taco Bell."*

Kids need freedom to make choices and sometimes even make mistakes. With or without your permission, they will choose which of their adventures to share with their loving, trusting parents. That's how the next generation learns responsibility.

On the other hand, there are all kinds of reasons why you need to keep the GPS option open. If there's terror in the streets. If your son or daughter consistently demonstrates they cannot be trusted. If two of their best friends get busted for possession. After losing their cell phone for the second time. After a certain number of traffic tickets or other run-ins with the law. You get the idea. And they will too.

Practically speaking, your wireless service provider and third-party tracking apps make this idea easy, affordable, and tempting. But please don't abuse the privilege.

The best way to keep the GPS option open is to engage in a semi-serious ceremony at the moment your child receives their first smartphone. Gather the family and present the sacred device in your most solemn tone of voice. Talk about the trust you are bestowing. Confirm that freedom brings responsibility. Explain how earned trust brings more freedom and loss of trust brings loss of privileges, earlier curfews, and . . . GPS installed on their precious phone. If they cross the line and force you to take that action, they will compare it to a house arrest ankle monitor. But tell them it's just for a month and, really, you have no desire to spend your evening tracking their every move.

Worth mentioning is that by installing a tracking app, you may be giving them the great gift of being able to say to their friends, *"I can't go to that party because of my ingenious parents and the GPS they put on my phone."* They may not thank you, but they will be glad you care.

Use the Needlepoint Metaphor

When your kids start questioning why God allows bad things to happen or sometimes doesn't make sense, feel free to quote Isaiah 55:8–9: "'For my thoughts are not your thoughts, neither are your ways my ways,' declares the Lord. 'As the heavens are higher than the earth, so are my ways higher than your ways and my thoughts than your thoughts.'"

Follow up with a little explanation. Maybe describe how God sees the past, present, and future all at once. He knows what's best. He loves us. We can trust him. Your curious child will nod, but may still not be completely satisfied.

That's when, if you have a cross-stitch or other needlework piece on the wall, you can become one of the great theological teachers of all time.

Turn that piece over so that the back faces your son or daughter. Ask what they see. Looking at the tangled zigzag of knots and loose threads, they won't be very impressed. If you did the needlework yourself, you can even express some disappointment that they don't appreciate all your hard work. That's when you turn it over to reveal a charming garden scene outlined by a few well-chosen words of wisdom.

Say something like "You see, the view from below is confusing. But the view from above makes perfect sense. The same thing happens when we compare our perspective with God's. Much of our messy lives are filled with loose threads, zigzags, and knots. Times when we have lost our way, changed our minds, and stopped in our tracks. But a heavenly perspective—one we cannot possibly have yet—reveals perfect order."

If your budding theologian is still listening, finish with this thought: "At the end of our lives, we'll see how God's handiwork comes together and makes perfect sense. Until then, we'll have to trust the Creator to keep crafting the story of our lives. Occasionally, we'll get a glimpse of his entire plan, but only if we look around and acknowledge the beauty and glory of this world he created to be our *temporary* home, until he takes us to our even more magnificent *heavenly* home."

Happy Everything

They appear almost magically. In mid-January, soon after the Christmas decorations get boxed up, a few subtle but noticeable embellishments appear on the shelves, walls, bureaus, and end tables of our home. That includes a plate decorated with a red heart, a curvy iron sculpture of the word *Love*, and most important, a glass heart-shaped candy dish filled with those little chalky-tasting conversation hearts.

In the Payleitner home, it's the work of the enchanting tradition-keeper I married named Rita. Hidden away in the corner of the basement, my bride has a stack of boxes marked Valentine's, St. Pat's, Easter, Fourth of July, Halloween, Thanksgiving, and Christmas. Each box contains things to remind us of the passing of time, underscore the importance of tradition, and tempt us with seasonal treats.

The mementos are more than just decoration. I believe those temporary seasonal ornamentations are a brilliant parenting strategy that helps make a house a home. Like warm cookies and cold milk after school, ever-changing holiday décor helps create a place of security and love that will keep kids coming home day after day, season after season, year after year.

21

Scrub Pots Together

I t's a classic parenting hack. Give them an assignment. And then join them in that task.

It's a win-win-win-win. The work gets done. You've lightened their load. You pass on hard-earned secrets regarding the best way to accomplish the task. (Some pots can go in the dishwasher, some pots need a little extra elbow grease, and some pots need soaking.) Best of all, you are working side by side to accomplish something together.

There's actually another term for scrubbing pots—or raking, dusting, sweeping, painting, folding laundry, cleaning the garage, or chopping wood—with your son or daughter. It's called doing life.

Stop Scrubbing Pots Long Enough to Make a Serendipitous Memory

One of the great rewards of working side by side with your children is the serendipitous moments that happen while pots get scrubbed, leaves get raked, garages get cleaned, and so on.

As you pull out a fresh towel to dry those pots, you realize that this particular towel was an heirloom from Aunt Marion, and you share a memory of helping her scrub pots after Thanksgiving at her home in Sheboygan Falls when you were nine years old. How did that old dish towel possibly end up in your cupboard?

This autumn, as you begin stuffing the twelfth leaf bag, you hear a familiar honking overhead. You hold up your hand and say, "Listen." And then you launch into some scientific speculation about how and why geese fly in a V formation. Ornithologists suggest it's for navigation and also to minimize wind resistance. If you watch long enough, you'll see that the lead goose changes every few minutes. Sure, you saw some geese fly over earlier that day, but what are the chances that another flock would fly overhead that afternoon, interrupting your raking project?

Next spring, as you and your garage-cleaning partner rummage through rusty hedge clippers, a box of slightly used spark plugs, and half-filled containers of old motor oil, you happen to come across a couple of classic orangish clay flowerpots. "Perfect," you say, "I just happen to have a packet of marigold seeds." So you take a break and tear open a bag of potting soil that you also just happen to have. Together you follow the directions on the seed packet. A week later, sprouts appear. In a month and a half, you have pots of marigold blooms. All because you just happen to invite your son or daughter to clean the garage with you. What are the chances?

Of course, sometimes moments that appear to be serendipitous aren't serendipitous at all. The word *serendipity* suggests that something nice happens simply by chance, which does transpire once in a while. God can certainly deliver an occasional nice surprise. But God also uses parents to orchestrate unexpected moments that have a good chance of making memories.

So go ahead and dig out an heirloom towel, time your yard work to coincide with a geese flyover, and buy some seeds and potting soil. I like to call it intentional parenting. In the moment—or years later—if they suspect you're hatching a sneaky scheme to make memories, go ahead and plead guilty. At worst, you'll be convicted of loving your family.

Insert Name Here

For each kid, ask God to give you a Bible verse. You can expedite the process by thinking and praying about each of your children. What are their gifts and passions? What might be their stumbling block in life? How can you best help them meet their God-given potential?

Dedicate a time of personal devotion and Bible study for each of your children. Memorize a portion of Scripture on their behalf. But here's what will make this strategy very real to you: One or two places, tuck their first name right inside that Bible verse. Here are five examples for you. My bride, Rita, has been praying these verses for our kids regularly for years.

I pray that Alec does not forget you, the Lord his God, by not keeping your commandments, your judgments, and your statutes which you command him today. I pray that Alec will remember the Lord his God, for it is you who give Alec the power to be successful. (Deuteronomy 8:11, 18, paraphrased)

I pray that Randy will remember whatever things are true, whatever things are noble, whatever things are just, whatever things are lovely, whatever things are of good report, if there is any virtue and if there is anything praiseworthy—that Randy will meditate on these things. (Philippians 4:8, paraphrased)

I pray that Max will wait on you, Lord, and that you will renew his strength. I pray that Max shall run and not be weary, and that he shall walk and not faint. (Isaiah 40:31, paraphrased)

I pray, Lord Jesus, that if Isaac abides in you and your words abide in him, that he will ask what he desires and it shall be done for him. (John 15:7, paraphrased)

I pray that Rae Anne will not be conformed to this world, but that she will be transformed by the renewing of her mind, that Rae Anne may prove what is the good and acceptable and perfect will of God. (Romans 12:2, paraphrased)

If you want to let the kids know you're praying for them, that's cool. But you don't have to. God will honor your consistent, persistent prayer either way.[1]

---

1. Portions excerpted from Jay Payleitner, *52 Things to Pray for Your Kids* (Eugene, OR: Harvest House, 2015), 148–150.

Make Room in the Fridge

ive kids is not a huge family. I remember growing up, the O'Keefes had ten kids and the Dillons had eleven. But in recent years, Rita and I often have had the most children of any family at sports banquets, block parties, extended family picnics, and church potlucks. Which means at the end of the event, the organizer would often say, "Jay and Rita, why don't you take home these leftovers?"

The first several times, I said, "Thanks, but no." But when I realized the sincerity of the offers and witnessed perfectly good food go to waste, I took a new approach. I came up with a line that has since served me well and may also work for you: "Thanks so much! All donations are appreciated."

Everyone benefits. The organizer feels generous and appreciated. The menu planner doesn't feel bad for ordering too much. The cleanup crew gets a helping hand. And the Payleitner family gets some Saran-wrapped fried chicken, pork chops, potato salad, brownies, and more.

There's no downside. So why do most people typically say no? Why do we so often put up walls that keep people from doing nice things for us? Are we cynical? Are we afraid of being beholden to someone? What's the worst that could happen? At a later date, someone may ask you for a favor? Oh no! Horrors! We might wind up doing something nice in return.

Really, we should learn and teach our kids to be gracious recipients of gifts and kind gestures. Every time we say "Thanks, but no," we isolate ourselves from being part of a community. That's tragic. By hardening our hearts to generosity we are cutting ourselves out of a chain of happiness.

The potential giver loses a chance to do something that brings someone else a nice dollop of happiness. And we miss out on giant cinnamon rolls, tickets to Wrigley Field, rides to the airport, and hand-knitted scarves.

One final note: When we finally learn to receive gifts graciously, there's a good chance we may enter a whole new level of gift-giving ourselves.

Repetitively Repeat
Important Lessons Redundantly

Imagine a nine-year-old boy at a pool party. Lots of splashing and diving going on. There happens to be an inflatable swimming ring floating about three feet from the edge of the pool. What's his core instinct? Dive through, right? That's a recipe for disaster. Seriously.

I've given the following little speech dozens of times and I'm not about to stop now. My kids all know it, but it bears repeating. Especially if there are young people in and around the pool who have not heard it.

Kids, listen up here for just a minute. There are not a lot of rules here. Mostly just common sense. But there's a story I need to tell you. And the moral is "no diving in the shallow end." See that swim ring? It looks like a perfect target to dive through, right? Well, a kid I went to high school with is paralyzed because he literally broke his neck diving into a shallow pool through a swim ring. So just be aware. Got it? That's all. Have fun.

Of course, there are a dozen other swimming pool safety rules, but kids know most of them by heart. Plus, they zone out during long lectures. It's also much more hospitable and effective to keep any group lecture short and pointed. What did they really hear during that ninety-word mandate? They heard that swimming pools are dangerous, and sometimes seemingly innocent activities can be life threatening. They heard there are expectations for how they act. They heard that Mr. Payleitner cares about their safety and future. And they heard that diving into swim rings is a bad idea.

A parental lecture is a tool that should be used rarely and judiciously. But when entering a dangerous or brand-new situation, you have the right and responsibility to expound, preach, and lay out serious ground rules. That includes any circumstance that involves firearms, fireworks, fishing hooks, medicines, extreme heights, motorized vehicles, gasoline, fire, whirling blades, swinging bats, chainsaws, axes, poisonous reptiles, bears, and perhaps the most inflammatory undertaking of youth: dating.

Call it a friendly reminder. Call it rules for life. A short redundant lecture from Mom or Dad is never a bad thing. If your precocious child whines, "You already told us this!" then it might even be a good idea to cancel the event. Or, at the very least, pull your kid aside and remind him of your role as vigilant parent and his role as respectful child. You can even quote Ben Franklin if you like: "An ounce of prevention is worth a pound of cure."

Let Them Set Their Own Video Game Boundaries

nchecked, some kids could spend ten hours a day playing video games. Even more on days when school is not in session. They would deny it, of course. If you accused them of engaging their controllers for a specific number of hours, you would be charged with exaggerating. Even if you pulled out a spreadsheet with specific times, locations, games, playing partners, and homework assignments missed, you still would not win the argument.

If you've come to such an impasse, you may need to play the "I'm the parent" card, which means you will need to set specific rules and limits. Things like no gaming on school nights or after nine p.m. No solo games. No playing for more than sixty minutes without a break.

Another way to reduce the automatic inclination some kids have to flip on their controller is to banish electronics on select family days like Christmas, Easter, Independence Day, Mother's Day, and other holidays important to your family. If you introduce those limitations, you'll want to plan worthwhile events that are even more fun than video games so "family days" don't feel like punishments.

Beyond deciding on time limits, parents also need to set limits on video game *content*. The ESRB (Entertainment Software Rating Board) has done a great service to moms and dads everywhere. The nonprofit, self-regulatory body assigns ratings for video games and apps. The six rating categories are Early Childhood, Everyone, Everyone 10+, Teen, Mature 17+, and Adults Only 18+. In addition, each ranking comes with content descriptors such as "blood and gore," "fantasy violence," "real gambling," "sexual content," and "drug reference." Like the more familiar movie ratings, sometimes you might disagree with or wonder about some of the rankings. But overall, it's still a valuable resource. The ESRB website keeps up with current releases and trends and even allows you to enter the title of games to check rankings before you allow your kids to participate.

Other issues to consider before turning your kids loose into this mind-numbing world are related to sharing the game console among siblings, earning hours through rewards and by performing extra household chores, and making sure that educational games are part of the mix.

Arguably, the best way to set limits is to have the kids set their own. That doesn't mean self-policing; parents still should expect to act as enforcers. But it does mean literally having the kids establish, codify, and write down when, what, and how many hours of video gaming may be played. The principle is this: Your kids think they only play a couple hours a day. They know you won't approve of games ranked "Mature17+" or even "Teen." Your growing kids also know that playing past nine or ten at night is a bad idea. So there's a good chance they will establish much stricter rules than you.

Given the chance, your intelligent eight-year-old son would probably propose, "Two hours a day, never past nine o'clock, ranking of 'Everyone 10+' and younger." You, of course, would be delighted with those limits, but don't tip your hand and jump into your happy dance. With a stern voice, promise that you will take their proposal, talk it over with your spouse, and get back with a counterproposal. Two days later, you say you will accept their terms, but with a couple of other limitations, such as "one day per week and certain family holidays will be designated as video-game-free," and other days their use is "only after homework is completed."

To make it official, you'll want to document these decisions so there is no confusion. Whether you have them sign the contract or post it on the refrigerator is up to you. You may also want to add a stipulation that certain grade-point averages must be maintained. Also, include a stipulation that you (Mom or Dad) can join in anytime and choose your own favorite game. Another part of the understanding that should almost go without saying is that aggressive behavior or cursing while playing will result in a weeklong ban. You may want to put that in writing as well.

One side benefit of having your kids set their own limits is that they're more likely to follow them and not try to get around the rules. Street-smart kids love to follow the letter of the law but break the spirit of the law. For instance, the agreement might indicate they cannot be playing a certain game at a certain time on their gaming console. What do they do? They play the same game on their phone. And that's legal, right?

Of course, if the original proposal by your young video game master is unreasonable, then you'll have to be firm with your counterproposal and stick to your guns.

Finally, Mom and Dad, remember that while your kids are setting the limits, you are still responsible for enforcing them. But now you can express it as more of a reminder than a command. After all, the limitations were all their idea.

Still, a nice kitchen-style timer might come in very, very handy.

27

Snap a Lost-Kid Photo

mmediately after entering into a theme park, museum, or giant shopping mall do a security review. Set some ground rules. Establish a meeting place if you get split up. Make sure cell phones are charged and on. Review the plan for meals, spending limits, and when you expect to call it a day. Then grab a group shot of your youngsters. If they get lost, you'll have an up-to-date photo, including exactly what they're wearing, to share with the local security officers.

The goal is not to frighten your kiddos. It's to let them know that even at the happiest place on earth, you are still protecting them and caring for their every need. They can count on you.

Everybody Out

With the goal of never being boring, may I suggest you be on constant lookout for reasons to stop the car and tell your kids to get out and stretch their legs. That could be at a roadsise attraction, scenic overlook, historical landmark, farmers' market, bald eagle nesting site, herd of buffalo, public garden, sculpture, boardwalk, or bridge.

You might think this kind of command would be limited to long-distance car trips. But part of our family lore is the time I gave that specific instruction to my whole family one nice Sunday afternoon on the way home from church.

Our park district had recently finished a beautiful walking bridge across the Fox River, and we were just about to drive under it. Instead, I pulled over and said, "Everybody out. I'll meet you on the other side." As you may suspect, my direct order was not met with immediate approval. My kids—ages four to seventeen—and my wife thought I was joking. I stood my ground and firmly repeated my command, "Everybody out. I'll meet you on the other side."

After a few groans and moans, the crew finally tumbled out of the minivan. As soon as they were clear, I sped away. I'm not sure what the conversation was as they walked up the rocky steps, over the bridge, and down the embankment on the other side. But the experience surely was not painful. As I said, it was a nice day.

The timing was perfect. I drove a half mile to the Main Street Bridge, through three busy intersections, pulling up just as they finished their not-so-daunting journey. Piling in, not one of them thanked me for the experience. I did hear one of the boys say, "You're crazy, Dad." I'll take that as a compliment.

All that to say, I totally recommend a few times a year pulling over at some amusing venue and saying, "Everybody out." You may or may not want to join them. Let me know how it goes.

The Simple Compliment

A few years back, all the business journals promoted a management principle nicknamed "The praise sandwich." The idea was to sneak some negative feedback between two positive statements. It might sound something like this: "Smedley, I really appreciate the research you gathered for the big presentation this morning. All the slides were upside down, you complete lunkhead. By the way, nice tie."

The problem with the formulaic praise sandwich is that the entire office catches on real quick. Every member of the staff learns that any compliment will be quickly followed by a slam. Pretty soon, even a sincere compliment will lead to cold sweats and heart palpitations. The receiver trembles with fear waiting for the reprimand that always follows.

In the same way, moms and dads want to avoid the praise sandwich or any parenting strategy that turns a positive into a negative. Why do we do that? Why do we so often keep talking after we compliment our children? "Hey, son, the lawn looks great. Did you sweep the grass off the sidewalk?" "Your coach said your footwork has really improved. Now you just need to start getting your first serve in." "Thanks for watching the baby. But you left the lid off the diaper pail."

Do you see how the follow-up comment invalidates the initial compliment? It leaves a bitter fog of negativity in the air. Instead, let's commit to making compliments that stick. In the examples above, it would be easy to just hack off that final sentence. If that's too tough, then replace it with another positive statement like "Well done" or "You're the best."

Go ahead and try giving simple compliments. Without any negative baggage attached. I know you can do it because you're a devoted and compassionate parent. Even though you often ignore good advice. (See what I did there?)

Never Just Walk by a Tree Stump

Taking walks with your kids is not a new breakthrough idea for moms and dads. Several good walks every week is the bare minimum for a parent and child of any age. The advantages of a good walk are self-evident. Exercise. Fresh air. Time away from screens. An extended time to talk about the opportunities and challenges of your child's current season of life. A chance to wave at neighbors and wonder at squirrels, armadillos, geckos, and other wildlife (depending on what part of the country you live in). And, of course, the opportunity to skip, hold hands, race to the corner, walk backward, pick a wildflower, or examine a spider web.

Something you may not always take full advantage of is a good tree stump. Let's consider three ways you can engage a tree stump you may happen upon.

First, take full advantage of said stump as an oratory platform. Moms and dads should step authoritatively onto any and all tree stumps and begin pontificating about the grandeur of the day and/or the magnificence of your traveling companion. Something like "Ladies and gentlemen, on this glorious autumnal afternoon, I present to you the one and only [insert child's full name here], the keeper of all wisdom, grace, and goodness. As he or she mounts this tree stump podium, I bid all creatures of the field and woods to welcome him or her with a well-deserved standing ovation." Now, of course, there is only a 50/50 chance your child will actually step up to the tree stump. Even then, his or her speech may or may not be an eloquent elocution. But, it's always worth a try. Even if you just get a sigh and a serious eye roll, your walk has still taken a fresh and memorable turn.

Another way to engage with a tree stump is to speculate with your young explorer how and why the tree was felled. Was it a victim of progress and new construction? Was it harvested for construction lumber, fine wood cabinetry, or paper pulp? Was it stricken with Dutch elm disease or wood rot? Or did it succumb to insect destroyers, such as the gypsy moth, tent caterpillar, or emerald ash borer? Did a homeowner order its removal because it dripped sap on her Ferrari or dropped leaves in his gutter? Make sure your conversation includes the question "Should we weep for the loss or celebrate the renewable resource of trees?"

A third option would be to count the rings. Among his many other scientific and artistic breakthroughs, Leonardo da Vinci is recognized as the first person to speculate that each ring represents a year and that the health of the tree during any growth season leads to a different thickness of the corresponding ring. I recommend you count back from the bark the age of your child to see what the growing season was like the summer they were born. And then count back another generation to find the ring established the year you were born. You may even be able to estimate the age of the tree and imagine what was going on "in this very spot" all those years ago. By the way, the scientific term for tree-ring dating is dendrochronology.

While many of the strategies in this book require forethought and planning, this one doesn't. Next time you're walking with your son or daughter, if you happen across a worthy stump, you'll know exactly what to do. Just trust your instincts (which might be to just keep walking).

Kids on Business Trips

Kids on business trips? I know what you're thinking. *Jay, you're kidding, right?*

No, actually I'm not. If business trips take you away from home on a regular basis, it only seems fair that some of those trips provide an occasional opportunity to bring your family closer. So, if and when it makes sense, take your kids—one at a time—on a business trip.

Of course, the stars have to be in perfect alignment. You can't just toss a child in your suitcase. And you can't expect the company to pick up the tab. Considerations must be made. First, it's a business trip, so your son or daughter should not distract from the business purpose of the travel. Also, when you're doing your "business stuff," your young traveling companion needs some kind of supervision. You'll want to get approval from your immediate supervisor and to double-check company policy. Then, be extra careful with your expense report. Your paperwork should closely resemble the expenses you submit on your typical solo trips.

One thing not to stress about is having your son or daughter miss a couple of days of school. I admit that early on, Rita and I never considered taking a child out of school for anything resembling a vacation. We even tsked parents who did such things. School was important! Skipping school devalued the entire educational process. It took a while, but we realized that our kids would learn more during an adventure with Mom or Dad than a routine week at school. (And really, teachers are pretty much fine with it.) Also, it was nice to be able to say, "Son, one of the reasons we can do this is because you're keeping your grades up."

If you're having trouble imagining your fourth-grader accompanying you on a boring routine business trip, allow me to describe the perfect scenario. Let's say you're scheduled to travel solo to Denver for a two-day conference. The required meetings are during the day and your evenings are free. Let's say it also just happens that a college friend (or a cousin, old neighbor, or work colleague) with a kid about the same age lives in the Denver area. With a phone call and some creative scheduling, you have a place for your son or daughter to hang out during those two days. As the pieces fall into place, you confirm schedules, book flights, and tie up any loose ends. You'll probably want to tack a vacation day onto the end of the trip so the two of you can see the Air Force Academy, ride a steam-powered locomotive, or drive up into Rocky Mountain National Park. Of course, you'll also want to show appreciation to your child's host by taking them out to dinner or inviting them to join you on your day trip. If this all sounds too complicated or costly, wait until a better opportunity comes along. But, please realize that making memories sometimes takes an investment of time and money.

Here's the point: It's typical for working dads and moms to put work in one box and family in another. Maybe you can create a win-win situation by occasionally comingling the content of those two boxes.

Buy a House With Sidewalks

O r *don't* buy a house with sidewalks. Either is fine. As long as you're thinking through your future living quarters with your kids in mind.

If it helps, imagine your family five or ten years from now and ask yourself what you're looking for when it comes to location. Or as real estate agents like to say, "Location, location, location."

Location, as in what city you choose. Is it family friendly? With parks, cultural activities, excellent schools, and vibrant churches? Is it near your extended family? Is the work commute so long that your early-evening dinners as a family are few and far between?

Location, as in what neighborhood you choose. Is it safe? Are there parks within walking distance? Are there other kids in the neighborhood? What specific schools will your kids attend?

Location, as in how kid-friendly is the actual piece of property. Where will your kids ride bikes and throw Frisbees? Can you imagine walking the sidewalks and waving to neighbors? Where will Rover run? Are cars zooming by at 50 mph? Will there be a lawn to mow, leaves to rake, and snow to shovel? (Those provide good opportunities for kids to learn responsibility.) When your kids are teenagers will your house be inviting to their friends? Where will you park that third car?

When house shopping, a majority of moms and dads will spend most of their time counting bathrooms, evaluating closet space, checking wiring, and worrying about real estate taxes. That's all important stuff. As for me, I totally recommend buying a house with sidewalks.

Back-to-School Night

Don't minimize the importance of Back-to-School Night. It can set the tone for the entire year for your student. Put that night on your calendar, Mom *and* Dad, and don't miss it.

Some parents shuffle in and out without many interactions. Others ask a slew of silly questions that don't matter or are already answered in handouts or online. Still other parents bring individual agendas to the evening or launch into their annual tirade of what's wrong with education in America.

I recommend you listen politely, sit a few rows back, and nod and smile a lot. Your mission is to read between the lines of everything that is being said or not said. Is this a well-organized, happy place? Do the teachers like their job? Is there a healthy hierarchy of respect for the principal and administration? Is there an oppressive amount of rules and ultimatums? Conversely, is there zero discipline and low expectations?

When the floor is open for questions, you'll probably have the chance to ask only one question. After dozens of back-to-school nights, I found one question that seems to reveal quite a bit about a teacher and his or her passion for what they do. "Mrs. Penny, what's your favorite part of the school year?" The answer may be, "All the units are important. I try to make them all interesting for the students." That's a boring response from a teacher who may have been teaching too long. Ideally, you want a teacher who lights up and begins talking passionately about something he or she cares about. Over the years, I remember a middle school science teacher answering my question by talking enthusiastically about timber wolves. It was fantastic. Another teacher spoke with passion about journaling and how she loves to see the progress in her students' writing skills through the year. Other teachers have spoken fervently about poetry, bats, the Colonial period, the 1960s, and local history. And it was my question that opened the door for them to talk about something they felt passionate about.

Back-to-School Night is actually a pretty big deal for teachers. They know how to handle students, but parents can be intimidating. That's all the more reason you want to put them at ease. Teachers remember parents who make their job easier and those who make their job more difficult. If you can, help them remember why they got into teaching in the first place.

Prepping for the Next Unit

E arly in the school year, see if you can snag an accurate schedule of what your student is going to be studying in the next nine months. Especially in science, social studies, and history. It could be readily available from the teacher. It could be posted online as mandated for the entire district. Or maybe it's a generic list that is only marginally helpful.

Don't race home and post that list on your fridge. Being forced to anticipate the entire school year might be a bit overwhelming for those elementary school students who are simply trying to get comfortable with a new teacher and classroom. Instead, file this information away for your own future reference.

The main reason parents should know what's coming up is so you can help give your kids a leg up. If you know they will be studying the Civil War, then gather the entire family to watch *Lincoln*, directed by Steve Spielberg. If you know they're covering astronomy the second semester, consider gifting your child with a telescope for Christmas. A well-timed trip to a children's museum may give your kids some nugget of information that finds its way into a classroom discussion. (Of course, don't tell your kids that you're helping them with their schoolwork.)

In addition, you need to know what's being taught because you may want to lay some groundwork in case your worldview doesn't match what they're being taught in the classroom. Controversial topics you'll want to monitor include evolution, sex education, alternative lifestyles, patriotism, free enterprise, gender studies, phonics, Christopher Columbus, immigration, and abortion rights. Perusing the year's curriculum, you may have to read between the lines to anticipate how any topic might be addressed.

To be sure, you shouldn't expect to change the entire approved curriculum. If you're up for the challenge, you can certainly take your case to the school administration and up the chain of command. Depending on your kids' ages, this might be an excellent opportunity to let them know that the Christian worldview is sometimes at odds with the secular worldview. But also make sure you tell them not to despair. After all, this world is not our final destination. As my pastor friend Steve Brown says, "We're not home yet."

35

Sock Rings

Rita and I have four sons. They were not allowed to put socks in the laundry unless they were matched and secured with sock rings. What's a sock ring? Google it. Sock rings, also sold as sock locks, just might be the greatest time-, frustration-, and money-saving devices in the history of the world. Especially if you have a house filled with athletes who wear three pairs of socks every day.

Doubling Productivity

Teach your kids to make efficient use of their downtime. Some examples:

Instead of perching like a drooling gargoyle in front of the microwave while waiting for their popcorn or oatmeal, tell them to make themselves useful. In ninety seconds, they could wipe down the kitchen counter, shake the crumbs out of the toaster, scrub a pot, or empty the top rack of the dishwasher.

While waiting for the bathtub to fill or shower water to get hot, how about making sure the top is on the toothpaste, hanging up a towel, straightening things on the countertop, or even replacing the empty toilet paper roll?

While waiting at the doorway for the dog to do his business, your youngster could bring in the mail, sweep the front porch, or actually notice and pick up the McDonald's wrapper that blew into your yard. Is that too much to expect? (Maybe.)

This lesson introduces your kids to the concept of doing two things at once. Which may lead into a spiritual conversation about 1 Thessalonians 5:17 (ESV), which tells us to "pray without ceasing."

That idea sounds impossible, until they understand that prayer doesn't require that you close your eyes and fold your hands. That's a wonderful submissive posture, but you can't go through life with your eyes closed. And prayer should be an ongoing part of everything we do.

Here's the point: Prayer allows your kids to be connected with the Creator of the universe at every moment of every day. (What a privilege!) Every time they punch the buttons on the microwave, turn on the shower, or let the dog out, they have the perfect opportunity for a quick prayer of gratitude. "Thank you for this food . . . thank you for hot water . . . thank you for Barkley."

When your kids learn they have the ability to pray without ceasing, suddenly they are not just doubling their productivity, they're discovering a new way of life. Even as they bike to the park, scan Netflix, spread peanut butter, clean the fish tank, or torment their little sister, they can be in constant communication with God. That goes beyond gratitude to include worship, confession, and seeking God's will. Your children will discover that consistent and constant prayer doesn't just double their productivity. It gives them access to the power that moves mountains.

The Slurpee Solution

You're attempting to drive while the kids are fighting, whining, punching, and pushing you to your limit. You could say something like "If you stop the ruckus, we'll get Slurpees (or Blizzards, Popsicles, or smoothies.)" That strategy may end the behavior, but it would also *reward* it. That's not a precedent you want to set.

Instead, try this terrific idea I spotted in Douglas Riley's parenting book, *Dr. Riley's Box of Tricks*. When a car trip becomes unbearable, don't say anything. But do pull your vehicle into the next 7–Eleven, Dairy Queen, mini-mart, or McDonalds. Tell the kids you'll be right back. Without any further conversation, get out of the car and come back with a single delicious kid-friendly treat . . . just for you. If you get back in the car, the whining will only get louder. So that's why you lean against the front fender and enjoy every sip and every slurp.

Finally, toss your empty cup or Popsicle stick into the trash receptacle and slide back into the driver seat. When the time is right, explain that you simply needed a break from the turmoil. You can even thank them for their patience. You can further explain that if they reduce their noise level, there's a reasonable chance you'll stop again and get treats for everyone! In an hour or two.

Basic, Basic, Basic Astronomy

A sk any number of well-educated adults why the moon appears as a crescent every month, and more than half of them will say, "It's the shadow of the earth."

Really. Try it. But please don't judge harshly. Those otherwise well-informed adults probably just never thought too much about it. It's true that sometimes the earth's shadow does fall across the moon, but that's called a lunar eclipse, which is a relatively rare event and should not be confused with the monthly lunar cycle.

Another basic, basic, basic astronomy truth your kids may not know is that the moon does not produce any light. Also, the moon orbits the earth. And also, the sun is a star. (Just a lot closer.)

These days, once kids have the basic ideas of a solar system and the rotation of the earth, they can look up all kinds of facts and statistics themselves. But parents, you can and should provide the basics before your kids embarrass themselves in a classroom or during a lunch table conversation.

Feel free to throw in this line of questioning, just to keep them thinking: "Which units of time were determined by God and which were human inventions?" Answer: The day and the year are dependent on creation. The earth rotates once a day and orbits the sun once a year. But ancient cultures—Egyptians, Babylonians, Chinese, Romans—are credited with dividing the day into twenty-four hours and the year into twelve months.

This discussion might also be a wonderful time to remind your kids of Psalm 8:3–4: "When I consider your heavens, the work of your fingers, the moon and the stars, which you have set in place, what is mankind that you are mindful of them, human beings that you care for them?" It's both humbling and comforting to consider how the Creator of the universe cares for each of us.

While we're on the topic. The seasons—winter, spring, summer, fall—are caused by the tilt of the earth's rotational axis at 23.5 degrees. A quick search online will help you explain how that works and also why the southern hemisphere (including Australia) is enjoying summer while the northern hemisphere is enduring winter. That should dispel the myth that the earth is closer to the sun during summer.

Mom and Dad, you don't have to be scientific gurus. But at the right time—on a camping trip or just looking up into the night sky—you should be able to offer your kids the basics of how the universe works.

39

Lunar Eclipse Lesson

Should you drag your second grader out onto the front lawn to see a lunar eclipse? At two a.m.? On a school night? My vote is "absolutely."

If she falls asleep at school the next day, her concerned teacher or classmates may ask her if everything is okay. That's when your young astronomer will yawn, smile, and say, "My mom and dad woke me up last night to see the lunar eclipse. It was so cool!"

The teacher will smile because he appreciates involved parents. The other students will all be jealous. And your son or daughter will remember that experience . . . forever.

Stress Not About Stuff That Just Doesn't Matter

When Alec was nine, I worried he would go through life with his hands stuck up inside the sleeves of his sweatshirt. It wasn't that his sweatshirts were too big. He just naturally withdrew his hand into his sleeves until the tips of his fingers were barely visible, if at all.

I actually lost sleep over it. I tried every parenting strategy I could think of to get him to walk with the cuff of his sleeves around his wrist. I asked him. I chastised him. I teased him. I reinforced the clean, well-groomed look of hands that were exposed to the light of day. I arranged for him to overhear me talking to his mom about how ridiculous it looked. I didn't punish or threaten him, because it wasn't evil or defiant behavior. It was just something that really, really bothered me.

Other than that one character flaw, Alec was the ideal son. Smart, respectful, handsome, athletic. But clearly this loathsome habit was destroying his entire constitution. He would never find a job. Never get married. Never find his way in this world.

And then one day it stopped. I'm not even sure I noticed it right away. I do recall that when I asked him about it, he had not really noticed either. It wasn't a habit he broke. It was a phase that phased out. Since then, my advice to parents when it comes to temporary conditions that probably won't last is to stress not. It's okay to be aware. But it's better to laugh it off. In other words, don't let a phase faze you.

Teach the Birds and Bees
Before Your Local Schools Do

I n Illinois, it's fifth grade. Which means that I needed to give the talk to each of my boys before that. And Rita had a similar private conversation or two with our daughter.

I believe the timing for school districts is motivated by the desire that no young ladies are surprised and panicked by their first menstrual period. That's a worthy goal. Fifth grade boys, of course, are all over the place when it comes to what they know, don't know, or think they know. Their surprise will come a few years later when about four out of five boys experience nocturnal emissions (aka "wet dreams").

Mom and Dad, you want your children first hearing about intercourse, erections, semen, fallopian tubes, and other such topics from you. Not some stranger or teacher who doesn't share your values.

The reasons for scheduling a preemptive sex talk are many. You don't want your fifth grader to faint, gasp, weep, or yell, "My parents never did that!" in the middle of their school day. You also don't want them feeling betrayed or ignorant. You do want to lay an informational foundation so they can come back to you anytime with questions.

Make a point to promote sex within a committed marriage relationship. The culture no longer supports that ideal. You should acknowledge that in the very near future many of their classmates may succumb to sex outside the marriage relationship. But the best time to explain how and why fornication and adultery fall outside God's best plan is before your children are overwhelmed with teenage hormones. While you have their full attention, you also have your best chance to clearly explain the benefits of the seventh commandment: "You shall not commit adultery" (Exodus 20:14).

Start by talking about how saving themselves until after their wedding will protect them from guilt, disease, pregnancy, comparisons with other partners, and heartbreak. But don't stop there. Explain how God has given them a beautiful expression of love to share one day with their husband or wife. The gift can only be opened once. The idea of giving yourself only to each other—forsaking all others—and discovering together what love really means as husband and wife is part of God's design. That's why the Bible teaches, "Marriage should be honored by all, and the marriage bed kept pure" (Hebrews 13:4). It's not just to protect you; it's to provide the kind of love that far too few couples experience.

While you're at it, you'll want to explain how God designed sex to create a permanent bond and celebrate love for wives and husbands. Point out Scripture passages such as "A man leaves his father and mother and is united to his wife, and they become one flesh" (Genesis 2:24) and "Rejoice in the wife of your youth. . . . May you always be captivated by her love" (Proverbs 5:18–19 NLT).

Then before the kids get all weirded out, you may want to get back to the part about how babies are made. Every new life is a blessing. God made humans in his image and has appointed us as caretakers of the earth. In the very first chapter of the Bible, it says, "God blessed them and said to them, 'Be fruitful and increase in number; fill the earth and subdue it'" (Genesis 1:28).

Most schools do a pretty good job of describing how the plumbing works. But they won't go much further than that. School districts no longer have any authority to place a moral judgment on when, where, and why people have sex. So, Mom and Dad, that lesson really is up to you. These days you'll want to share these conversations with a degree of intentionality, probably earlier than you may have considered.

One final note: You have to feel sorry for young people who grow up without understanding the spiritual side of sexual intimacy. They are destined to miss out on something wonderful. Sex is a gift from God to be opened at just the right time. Make sure your kids know that.

Be the Bad Guy

You're doing a pretty good with job with your kids. They're developing their own moral compasses. They know right from wrong. They are really embracing what you're teaching. Give yourself a pat on the back.

However, while they're trying to stay true to those worthy values, they're also trying to make friends and not be labeled a goody-goody or worse.

As they begin to own their own convictions, they will eventually figure out the right words to stand up to peer pressure. But for now you have the duty and privilege of giving them a few gifts. Things like curfews, boundaries, and family rules. Your fifth grader doesn't want to smoke, drink, huff, vandalize, shoplift, get high, skip school, moon a cop, or go cow tipping. Still, if they have a social life, there may come a season or a summer or just an evening, during which they find themselves associating with a group of kids who are doing some or all of those not-so-appropriate activities.

Even if you're not there, you still have a chance to rescue them. On a regular basis, let them know how awesome they are. Tell them you are so glad you can trust them. Acknowledge that there are plenty of temptations out there. Name a few. Keep lines of communication open with neighbors, teachers, coaches, and other parents about what's going on in your community. You may even want to ask your kids about current trends. "Are kids still smoking in middle school?" "I heard that police are cracking down on alcohol in the forest preserve." "I saw a news report on kids sharing prescription drugs. Is that a real thing?"

When faced with a bit of peer pressure or temptation, your nonjudgmental voice will be echoing in their minds. They will be grateful they have a curfew. It's a convenient excuse. It's more proof that boundaries are good things.

Offer yourself as chief bad guy. Tell them to blame you. "My dad would kill me." "My mom would freak out if she thought I was smoking." "My folks would find out. They always find out." "I have to be home by eleven." "My parents make me check in before leaving parties or school events." They may never thank you, but it's worth it.

And if your son or daughter ever does go cow tipping, insist that you be invited. Sounds like fun.

"I Think You're Done for the Day"

Your son curses at whatever is on his phone. Your daughter insists she can't set the table because she's texting with her BFF. Three times, your first grader doesn't respond to a simple question because he's mesmerized by some cartoon on television. A friendly game of Settlers of Catan has turned not so friendly. A game of driveway basketball has turned into a shouting match complete with some totally inappropriate language from your child or a friend. The new driver rolls through a stop sign. Go ahead and use those seven easy-to-pronounce words: "I think you're done for the day."

The screen is powered down. The phone confiscated until morning. The board game, basketball, or car keys are tucked away.

It's not a punishment. Your wonderful children really haven't done anything terribly evil. It's just that they need a reboot. They need an attitude adjustment. They need to understand that screens, phones, driving, sports gear, and many other things they take for granted are not rights but privileges.

Don't allow them to howl about fairness. (Life isn't fair.) Certainly don't allow them to ignore your seven-word behest (I think you're done for the day). They will—they must—comply. Your words need to be respected. After all, your response is not overboard or oppressive. You didn't yell, "No TV for a month!" You didn't sentence them to years of hard labor. You're not even telling them what to do. You're not raising your voice at all.

The next morning or afternoon, their possessions and privileges are returned. If they're not grateful, you may want to reassert your authority for another day.

Go ahead and practice saying it right out loud: "I think you're done for the day." Like so many parenting tactics, this one works best when you start early, practice consistency, create a sense of partnership, and gain consensus with your parenting partner.

Clean Stuff Besides Dishes in the Dishwasher

Flip-flops. Sneakers. Baby toys. Sandbox toys. Swimming goggles. Hairbrushes. Combs. Dog chew toys. Sponges. Toothbrushes. Toothbrush holders. Mouth guards. Wiffle balls.

Even baseball caps. But you'll want to invest in a plastic ball cap washer to make sure it keeps its shape. You can get them for less than ten bucks. Follow the directions, especially being sure not to wash ball caps and any other fabric items with dirty dishes.

Amusement Park Hacks

Don't just walk up, pay full price, and walk zombie-like for the day. A little homework and strategic thinking can go a long way toward saving time, saving money, minimizing aggravation, and maximizing your amusement park experience.

Buy tickets online. Choose dates wisely. Arrive at the park early. Don't follow the crowds. If a crowd goes right—which people instinctively do—you go left. Take digital pix of your parking lot location. Bring small Ziploc bags to protect your phones during water rides.

Take advantage of the latest apps and park services. Consider multi-day passes, staying on-site, and tickets that allow for line jumping. The extra cost may actually be offset because you can see more stuff in fewer days. Apps can make reservations, estimate waiting times, locate park secrets, suggest shortcuts, and even locate mascots and characters strolling through the park. Follow the park Twitter account, which might offer other hints, discounts, and surprises.

Other commonsense tips for amusement parks are to stay hydrated, carry granola bars, wear sunscreen, decide on a few must-do rides and events ahead of time, and secure your wallets.

Some websites and amusement park experts recommend that families split up so that everyone gets to do the stuff they want to do. But really? Sharing the day and making memories as a family is worth missing one or two rides. Don't you think?

Homeowner Secrets

There are a ton of things you take for granted that would be empowering to a nine-year-old. That includes stuff you learned so long ago that you don't even know you know.

Examples? How to reset the circuit breakers. How to shut off the main water supply to the house. How to stop the toilet from running. How to change the furnace filter. How to silence a squeaky door hinge. How to clear dryer lint. How to use a plunger. How to change a light bulb. How to change a light bulb when the glass has shattered and just the metal base is left in the fixture. How to open the fireplace flue. How to unjam the garbage disposal. You get the idea.

When a child of elementary school age learns one of these household maneuvers, they feel like they've been invited into the inner circle. They've been entrusted with knowledge not available to unenlightened and unworthy younger children. This is grown-up stuff.

Please note the above list does not include wallpapering a bedroom, tiling a kitchen floor, replacing a screen door, or assembling IKEA furniture. Those are potentially grueling jobs that typically require advance planning, multiple trips to the hardware store, and unwelcome troubleshooting along the way. Feel free to recruit your *teenager* to partner with you in those tasks.

The allure of these seemingly mundane tasks is the *revelation*. There's a magical quality to it. These are skills a child does not have. Ten minutes later, they do. Presented properly—perhaps with a bit of a whisper—the experience can be profoundly satisfying to a curious child.

The best part about this initiation into homeowner secrets is that you don't have to schedule these lessons. They happen naturally in the course of a year. When something around the house needs fixing, replacing, cleaning, or plunging, simply invite your young assistant to inspect the problem and witness the solution.

Yes, the four-minute job has now become a seven-minute job, but isn't it worth three minutes of your life to give your child such a gift? Send them on their way with a hearty hail of appreciation for their assistance and there's a good chance they will join you in a few years for a more grueling job when you really do need their help.

Visit Colleges

You've taken your grade schooler to the zoo, haven't you? Depending on where you live, regular zoo visits are almost mandatory. Sure, kids can watch a larger-than-life lion chase a wildebeest across the savannah in an IMAX theater. But there's no comparison to seeing a real living, breathing king of the jungle. Even if all the big cats do is lounge, purr, and pace.

But have you taken them to a college or university campus? Consider the parallels. Both venues feature specific boundaries with buildings old and new. Odd creatures and wildlife appear on every corner. There are lots of trees, walking paths, special events, custom living quarters, a flow of new residents, and posted feeding times. Signage and posters offer a wide range of information that may require some explaining to a younger audience. There's much to see and even more to spark the imagination.

Next time you're considering a zoo trip, consider instead wandering around a university campus with your family. Or go to a scheduled event. Experience the pageantry of a football game or a smaller athletic contest. The arts are well represented on most campuses in the form of theater, concerts, arts shows, and recitals. If you're respectful, you can wander in many open doors. Not the dorms. But the library, student center, chapel, and most academic buildings are typically open to the public during the school year.

The goal is to spark your child's imagination. Each door you literally open could figuratively open a new door in a young student's life. You've already told them, "You can be anything you want to be." Achieving such an ambitious goal requires key moments of self-discovery, and those happen daily on college campuses around the world.

As you walk between buildings—and for days after—expect some surprising questions and lively conversations. Or your child may be awestruck. By the size. The possibilities. The responsibilities. The decisions to be made.

Your child also may be unsettled or not quite ready to think about himself as a young adult. A visit to a university campus is a chance to plant seeds and notice their young minds churning as they ponder their hopes and dreams. Leave your pen and notebook in the car. But take plenty of mental notes regarding what piques their curiosity and how you can nurture those ruminations.

Finally, make sure you get back to the car before they get bored or start complaining their feet hurt. You want to leave them wanting more.

Personalized Pancakes

Fill a turkey baster with pancake batter and squeeze any free-form shape you can imagine onto your hot griddle. Hearts. Bunnies. Christmas trees. Clovers. Smiley faces. Letters. Names. Xs and Os.

Younger kids will be thrilled. Older kids will not be quite as exuberant. But they will secretly appreciate it, perhaps even more than their younger siblings.

Your Response to Their Frustrations

When faced with a challenging assignment or project, every kid is different.

Your pessimistic child states, "I can't do this." Your perfectionist says, "I'll never get this right." Your go-getter vows, "I can do this, but I need more time." Your slacker moans, "Do I have to do this?" Your thoughtful kid considers, "Where should I start and how long do I have?" Your procrastinator declares, "I'll do this tomorrow."

Good news. You can address all these scenarios with this comforting promise from Philippians 1:6: "I am certain that God, who began the good work within you, will continue his work until it is finally finished on the day when Christ Jesus returns" (NLT).

Theologians will tell you this verse applies specifically to our spiritual lives. God's work on our behalf began on the cross and continues in our lives as we accept grace, trust him, and listen to the Holy Spirit. Once we begin our journey of faith, he's going to make sure our work is finished at just the right time. His timing, not ours.

Similar passages confirm that God wants us to finish what we start. "My only aim is to finish the race and complete the task the Lord Jesus has given me" (Acts 20:24). "I have fought the good fight, I have finished the race, I have kept the faith" (2 Timothy 4:7).

I think you'll agree that the goal of finishing strong extends beyond exclusively spiritual matters. God wants our kids to face the challenges of life with confidence and perseverance. Tackling academic, athletic, extracurricular, physical, and relational goals allows our kids to sharpen their tools for future endeavors. Many of which will bring glory to God.

So when your favorite young contender looks at a task and hesitates, vows, moans, whines, or declares, you've got a few ways to respond, right from Scripture: "God began this and he will continue to work in you and through you." "Finish the race." "Fight the good fight." "Keep the faith." Also tell them, "Win or lose, you've got parents and a heavenly father cheering you on."

Pegs

Clothes hangers and grade schoolers don't go together. Especially when it comes to clothes that have been worn once but don't quite yet require laundering.

You can insist they hang virtually clean articles of clothing back in the closet, but when it doesn't happen, do you really want to fight that battle? How about setting everyone up for success? You're not giving in to their grumbling or careless ways. You're simply choosing a better option.

Somewhere in their room install a line of pegs or hooks at a child-friendly height. They can be decorative or purely functional. They can be behind a door, in the back of the closet, or right out in the open. Mount these pegs right onto the drywall or part of a long wooden rack or large pegboard.

Then firmly establish the new house rules. If it's never been worn, it's on a hanger. If it's been worn but can be worn again, it goes on a hook. If it's dirty, it goes wherever dirty clothes go. Easy. No clothes piled on the floor or bed ever again.

If you have enough hooks, reserve one or two for towels, robes, and even a book bag. But if all the hooks are full, that's still no excuse for clothes on the floor. Alternately, you could pick up a kid-sized coat rack that takes up a minimum of floor space.

On the topic of laundry, there will come a time when every child—girls and boys—needs to pretty much be responsible for their own laundry. The problematic challenge is, when that becomes a house rule, some kids will wear the same jeans forty days in a row without washing them. In that case, I recommend you snag those filthy jeans in the middle of the night, do a single load of laundry, and return them neatly folded with a sticky note that says something like "These jeans started to crawl down the hallway, so I pounced on them and washed the alien life force out of them. Love, Mom."

Field Trip Frugality

Proverbs 21:20 (NLT) says, "Fools spend whatever they get." Now, I'm not calling your kid a fool, but there's a high probability that if you give your son or daughter twenty bucks for an outing or field trip, they're going to spend every nickel. Can you blame them?

Jonathan Clements, wealth management consultant and former columnist for *The Wall Street Journal*, suggests a strategy for countering this prodigal behavior. It requires no lecturing and your kids will learn to be wiser with money all by themselves.

The basic idea is to "make your kids feel like they're spending their own money."[1] Before your nine-year-old goes on a class field trip, they are going to ask you for lunch and spending money. Dutifully, you slip an Alexander Hamilton or Harriet Tubman out of your wallet. But don't just give it to them and say, "Have a good time." They won't think twice about spending your hard-earned cash, and you will have reinforced the perception that money grows on trees. Also don't say, "Bring me back the change." For sure, they'll keep spending until it's gone and you'll be lucky to get back thirty-seven cents.

Instead, look them in the eye and say, "This is now your money. It's my gift to you. Whatever you don't spend on the field trip is yours for something you may need or want later. Have a great time. I want to hear all about it when you get home." At the cafeteria, your sharp child will dine sensibly. When they get to the museum gift shop, they'll think twice before buying

---

1. Jonathan Clements, "Making Kids Money Savvy: Try These Four Financial Tricks," *Wall Street Journal*, March 4, 2008, http://www.wsj.com/articles/SB120468099339812197.

the dust-collecting plastic dinosaur or genuine artificial Native American tomahawk made in China.

If they save a few bucks, that's great. In a sense, they've earned it. If they blow it all that day, there's a good chance they'll have a twinge of regret and come away with a real-life lesson that will serve them well for years to come.[2]

2. Excerpted from Jay Payleitner, *10 Conversations Kids Need to Have with Their Dad* (Eugene, OR: Harvest House, 2014), 109.

Asking for Kid Insight

You want your kids—eventually—to know things you don't know and do things you can't do. Otherwise, there will never be any reason for them to identify their own God-given purpose in this world and . . . move out. But that's years away, right? They could not possibly have any helpful ideas or insights applicable today, could they?

What could that slightly goofy-looking child with matted hair, a quizzical expression, mismatched clothes, muddy shoes, disgusting eating habits, and zero understanding of your grown-up world possibly do for you? I have no idea. But you might be surprised.

Consider for a moment a few of the life challenges you are facing right now. A dilemma, irritation, obstacle, or can of worms you have to deal with in the next several minutes or several weeks. It may be at work, home, play, or church. It may involve communication, technology, leadership, media, parenting, some personal interaction, whatever.

What if you ask your kid for help? Really. What if you say something like "Hey, I could use your help on a project. Do you have a few minutes?" Then treat them like an adult colleague in a work environment. Lay out your problem in simple terms and encourage their questions. In the give-and-take, use creative brainstorming principles, such as "no judging" and "piggyback on each other's ideas."

Undoubtedly, some of their questions or input will be way off target. But—with your bright, curious offspring—I'm thinking you may actually gain a new perspective you might be able to use. Need examples?

- You may be planning to rip out walls in order to hardwire a connection between two systems, but your tech-savvy kid may recommend you go wireless.

- Lunchtime with the toddler twins has turned into a peanut butter battle because one wants crunchy and the other creamy. Your eight-year-old daughter suggests you simply buy two jars.

- You've been charged with updating the company newsletter. Your young genius may recommend some new interactive elements, streaming video links, infographics, a rewards program, an element of interoffice competition, or simply a new font or color.

- At work, company history dictates hiring an impossible-to-find V.P. of Development equipped with both editorial and technology skills. Your child offhandedly suggests you hire two part-timers instead.

- Your architectural landscaping firm is preparing to pour sidewalks in a perpendicular grid at the new office complex. Your son or daughter recommends you wait a few months to see what paths are worn in the grass by the foot traffic of building tenants. That info reveals exactly where to install permanent walks.

You get the idea. But get ready for this slightly infuriating twist. Let's say you take your kid's idea and run with it. It's well-received at all levels. High fives for everyone. Of course, during implantation, there are some tweaks to the original concept, but that's the way the world works. As an adult, you know that. But when you reveal the final outcome to your son or daughter, the response is inevitable: "That's not what I said. You ruined my idea."

Oh well. That's a fresh chance for you to give your child another glimpse into the world of compromise and working as part of a team.

How to Convince Your Son
He Needs a Haircut

Really? Do you really think the length of your son's hair is important? There are six million things more important than the length of your son's hair. As the author of this book, I will not dedicate a single page to strategies about getting your son to cut his hair.

On the other hand, strategies for getting him to open up and talk about his hopes and dreams are worth exploring. Mom and Dad, any time you spend trying to manipulate his choice of hairstyle would actually be counterproductive to that more important goal.

So, how do you prompt healthy conversations about hopes and dreams with your kids? That's really the focus of this entire book. It's about entering their world. Advocating for them on occasion. Setting them up for success. Helping them set expectations. Laughing together. Introducing them to Jesus. Stimulating their creativity. Earning their trust.

So come alongside your son and help him see the wonderful opportunities that await him. If one of those opportunities requires that he cut his hair, then he will. On his own. But for some of those opportunities, longer hair is actually a benefit—rock star, fashion model, artist, college professor, barista. (You get the idea.)

Don't make your son cut his hair. You *can* make sure he cleans out the shower drain. You *can* ask him to pitch in for the vast amounts of shampoo and conditioner he uses. You *can* even joke about his hair. But your constant goal should be to make sure that after every conversation he has with you, he is glad to have had it. You have two choices. Either push him away. Or pull him toward you.

Envision Your Kids As Parents

On any occasion when you want to strangle your child, don't. It may help to ask yourself this question: *"Someday, do I want to have grand-kids and be an important part of their lives or not?"* That answer may help you get through any short season of frustration.

Camping Out in the Bathroom

lu bug going around? For moms and dads, first pray that at least one of you can clean up puke without succumbing to your own gag reflex. In our home, that's me. When the worst moments of stomach flu season hit, I'm the hero of the realm. Rita has put me in charge of all cleaning up as well as minimizing the need for cleaning up. As you might expect, she's very appreciative.

At this point, I feel the need to apologize to those of you who may even start to gag a little when the topic is brought up. If you're inclined to skip this chapter, that's actually an indication that you need to keep reading.

When the bug hits, there are two primary goals. First, get 100 percent of all vomit directly into the toilet. Second, don't make the child—who's already suffering—feel bad for being sick. These two goals are closely related. Because if your child doesn't make it to the bathroom in time, upchucking all over the hallway walls and carpet, they will feel terrible and you will be more than a little upset and frustrated with the entire episode. It's an undeniable lose-lose situation. Not to mention the hallway carpet is going to smell nasty for weeks or months.

So here's what you do. Stay vigilant. If you know the flu bug or food poisoning is imminent, anticipate that one of your kids may become the next victim. Explain the symptoms: queasiness, sweats, rumbling tummy, shivers, and that foreboding feeling that something in your gut doesn't want to stay there. Then stress your main goal. If at all possible, *puke in the toilet.*

Here's the key to successfully accomplishing that goal. Tell them once they start to puke there's no way they can possibly make it to the bathroom in time. (Which is, of course, true.) So . . . they need to *be there already.*

That's right. Day or night, your maybe-about-to-puke kid should be camping out on the bathroom floor. Make it a bit of an adventure. While they sit ashen-faced and nauseated, you should spread out three or four beach towels or fold an old comforter in half on the floor. Roll up another towel for a pillow. Depending on the age of the child, Mom or Dad, you might want to make a bed for yourself right outside the bathroom door.

Is this overkill? Is it really necessary to totally sacrifice the comfort and sleep of two family members just because a child is a little queasy? The answer is yes. If you've ever scrubbed vomit out of a bedroom or hallway carpet, you wouldn't even be asking that question.

There's really no need to go much further here. If a child does spring up and reach for the toilet, you will want to do all of the appropriate forehead holding, mouth rinsing, and soothing vocal encouragement. Let them know the first round is the most aggressive, but there will most assuredly be a second and third round within a few minutes. Explain how it's just their tummy emptying out the bad germs and everything else inside. When it's over, they will feel much, much better.

If they partially miss the bowl, that's really okay. Cleaning the bathroom tile is a breeze compared to the rest of the house. If it's a false alarm and no one does any puking, that's a good thing, right?

If you're lucky, by third grade or so, your child will recognize the signs and stay in close proximity to the toilet. But no matter what, don't make your kid feel guilty for something over which they have zero control.

Oh, and if you're the one who stays far away while your husband or wife takes charge of the flu epidemic, express your gratitude early and often. Rita, you're welcome.

Expectations and Disappointment

oday's culture suggests that it's wrong to express expectations or disappointment with your kids. As if we're putting too much pressure on them. Or setting them up for failure. Hogwash.

Our expectations for our children establish goals, which actually set them up for future achievement. When a parent expresses disappointment, we're letting our kids know they have talents and abilities that have not yet been harvested. We're expressing our belief that their future includes daring new feats and meaningful masterpieces. We're letting them know the world is counting on them to pursue and fulfill their destiny.

God himself has great plans and high expectations for his followers: "No eye has seen, no ear has heard, and no mind has imagined what God has prepared for those who love him" (1 Corinthians 2:9 NLT). Does that statement prompt stress? Or is it exciting and empowering to consider what the future might hold?

Jesus expressed disappointment without apology to a small group of individuals he thought he could count on. In Matthew, chapter 26, he asks Peter, James, and John to stand firm with him during the most crucial night of his life. That evening he had already washed feet, broke bread, shared wine, fully explained his earthly mission, and identified the two men who would betray and deny him. Heading into the garden of Gethsemane, he turns to his three closest friends and says, "My soul is crushed with grief to the point of death. Stay here and keep watch with me" (Matthew 26:38 NLT). All he wanted was for these guys to stay awake for sixty minutes. They didn't do it. And Jesus let them know he was disappointed. "Then [Jesus] returned to the disciples and found them asleep. He said to Peter, 'Couldn't you watch with me even one hour?'" (Matthew 26:40 NLT).

It's worth noting that after a few more false starts, Peter, James, and John took their assignments seriously, becoming leaders of the early church and together writing eight books of the New Testament.

So don't hesitate to set a high bar for your children. They just may meet or surpass your expectations. Continue to let them know you love them unconditionally and will never give up on them. That's why you can share their disappointment when they fall short of a reachable goal.

Nine Times Anything

D o kids still memorize multiplication tables? I hope so. It's not a true indicator of math prowess. But it's a task that can be mastered and has application to real life. Sure, a calculator is never far away these days, thanks to our phones. But being able to do simple math in your head allows you to move through life with some sense of proportion, quantity, and allotment.

"Eight rows of twelve chairs. That's almost a hundred people!"

"If he can play five more years averaging thirty home runs, he's going to pass five hundred. And that should get him into Cooperstown."

"If every girl sells thirty boxes, we'll beat last year's troop record."

"There's six in your family and seven in my family. If everyone takes six Tater Tots . . . sixty is not nearly enough!"

Whether we're setting goals, distributing donut holes, installing bookshelves, or hiding Easter eggs, basic math skills come in real handy.

Here's the best math trick I know. It's an instant way to memorize the *nine times table*. In other words, nine times any single digit number. Here goes. Let's take nine times seven. Ask yourself, "What is one less than seven?" The answer is six. Then ask yourself, "What's the difference between that number—six—and nine?" The answer is three. So nine times seven is 63. With a little practice, this should happen instantly in your head. One more example. Let's take, nine times three. What is one less than three?

Two. What's the difference between two and nine? Seven. So nine times three is 27. You can confirm your answer by adding up the two digits. The sum should always be nine. Let's take a quick look at all the answers in the nine times table: 9, 18, 27, 36, 45, 54, 63, 72, 81, 90. See the pattern? You may not, but your sharp second grader will!

58

Sibling Math Races

Competition between siblings (or cousins) is a great tool for parents. While you can still outsmart them, there are all kinds of ways you can use competition to take advantage of your kids and they won't even know it.

Got a pile of bricks that need to be moved from here to there? On your mark, get set, go. Winner gets an extra scoop of ice cream. To make it fair, you can weight the number of bricks according to age and ability. Maybe the younger sibling gets to count each brick twice. If the brick carriers are fairly close in age, maybe the results are weighted three to two. Or four to three. Suddenly the brick race also turns into a math exercise. The goal is to give any and all the kids a chance to win. (And to get those bricks moved.)

For a while, the principle might also work with other projects that need doing. Got a laundry basket of socks to be matched? Or how about racing to finish shoveling their portion of the driveway or raking their half of the lawn? Add penalty seconds for a sloppy job.

One of my favorite bedtime games was the sibling math race. This works with any two or even three kids, even when they're in different classes. Each round begins when the moderator (that's you) says two single-digit numbers. For instance "Seven, five." The younger child has to add them together: "Twelve." The older child has to multiply them: "Thirty-five." The even older child might have to square the numbers, and then add them. "Seventy-four." It may sound unlikely, but sibling math races can get quite amusing. Especially when you start using fractions, negative numbers, numbers with multiple digits, and so on.

Be warned, you will definitely hear squeals of "That's not fair!" Especially when you slowly begin to say the next two numbers, "Zero . . ." If you don't know why that's funny, you need to review your third grade math.

59

The Art of Pausing

Two, maybe three, generations ago, children were taught to stand when an adult entered the room. Well, let's not push our luck to insist on that old custom. But way before our kids reach the totally self-absorbed teenage years, let's make a collective parenting pledge to teach the art of pausing to the next generation.

It shouldn't be that big of a deal. Just about every video game, television, and audio playback device has a button that actually says the word *Pause* or has that little vertical equal sign (which means *Pause*).

When Mom or Dad walk through a room, we really don't want our kids to immediately stop what they're doing and jump to their feet. But if we do stop in their line of vision and meet their gaze, every kid should know they have just received a clear signal to pause. Without any hint of a grimace, that young gamer or TV watcher needs to hit the pause button, look up, and acknowledge your presence with actual words.

Don't abuse the privilege. Don't embarrass them in front of their friends. But do make it clear—maybe in a short conversation specifically addressing this new house policy—that their undivided attention is something that you require once in a while, even if it's not convenient for them at the moment. This is not a battle or ultimatum or punishment. It's a form of respect.

Worth noting: In general, parents should also be expected to practice the art of pausing when a respectful child has a question or need. Exceptions to this rule may include the final moments of a championship sporting event or the climatic scene in the first viewing of a major motion picture.

Oil Their Mitt

I love coaching baseball and softball with kids at ages eight to nine. They're starting to get some skills, but they still know they have much to learn. In a few years, they will think they know more than you do. After coaching that age of boys and girls for more than a dozen years, I have come to one significant conclusion: It's almost impossible to catch a ball with a new baseball glove.

At the beginning of the season, one or two players always show up with a glove purchased that very day. It might be a legit, high-end model. But the leather is as stiff as a board, not broken in, and has no snap. The best thing a mom or dad can do—days before that first practice—is grab a bottle of leather oil and follow the instructions.

Oh yeah, it wouldn't hurt if you got them out in the side yard or street and played a few games of catch as well.

Be Smart With Smartphone Photos

When my kids were growing up, I would whip out my wallet to show a half dozen family photos every chance I got.

I would start with the photo of Rita and me on our third date. It was high school prom 1975. Me in an all-white tuxedo. Rita in a modest, flowing, pale green dress with dozens of partially clothed water nymphs on it. She had purchased the dress and put it on for the dance without even noticing the faint images in the fabric. But her stepfather noticed. As she was walking down the stairs to greet me, he said, "You can't wear that dress; there are naked ladies on it." Thankfully, Rita's mom saw the humor, overruled her husband, and the story is now part of our family lore.

The other photos were mostly wallet-size school pix that tended to embarrass the kids. They were typically not very flattering, but the choice of pictures that fit in my pocket was pretty limited back then.

Today the problem is the exact opposite. When someone asks to see photos of their kids, many parents—dads especially—have a hard time finding good shots because there are hundreds of photos on their smartphone. Including photos of landmarks, shopping lists, household projects, recipes, prescription bottles, and pets. Plus, way too many bad selfies.

In the moment, it's impossible to sift through hundreds of photos to find decent pix of your kids, so you don't. Which means you miss out on the chance to brag a little and confirm to a friend or colleague that you cherish your role as a parent.

So here's what you do: In your photo app, create one album called *FOR SHOW*. Keep *fewer than a dozen* photos in it. Only the best of the best. Select clear, charming pix that show off your family members in fabulous poses doing fabulous things. Anytime the occasion arises, you can open that album and invite a friend to swipe though a limited number of photos. While they're swiping, you don't even have to look. You know that the photo of Amy in her tutu comes right after the photo of Joel and Karla with the new baby. Friends and acquaintances will hand back your phone and always says the same thing: "That's a great-looking family."

It's not painful or prideful. The whole process takes less than a minute. Actually, it's a win all the way around. If you see me at an airport, convention, or men's event, stop and ask to see my "pictures for show." I'll show you mine, if you show me yours.

62

Responding When They Fail

I t's one of the great challenges of parenting. How should you respond when one of your kids fails? What do you do when their best effort doesn't match their goals?

You want them to get back on the horse. You want them to tough it out and try, try again. But you also know that sometimes the right thing to do is to take a step back and not push too hard. Maybe your daughter isn't going to be an Olympic gold medalist like Jennie Finch or Lindsey Vonn. Maybe your son isn't going to be a state champion wrestler or make the PGA tour. Some kids really are tone deaf. Some people just can't do math in their head. You can't force an introvert to be an extrovert. Soufflés fall. Kids get cut from teams.

Should you push? Or encourage your child to shift their efforts to a new path?

First, let them react. They may want to vent or cry or even express a little anger with themselves or the situation. In the moment, your job is to just listen.

Second, don't make any rash decisions. You . . . or them. Don't let them throw their golf clubs in the pond. Don't threaten the referee. Don't yell at the coach. And—in the heat of the moment—don't let them quit the team.

Third, keep gathering information. That's really an ongoing responsibility of any parent in the audience or on the sidelines. The only way you'll know whether your son or daughter should keep pursuing any endeavor is by being invested in the day-to-day routine. If you just show up at the final match or end-of-season competition, then you have no idea what to expect. When they come up short—or even if they experience victory—you'll feel out of the loop and ill-equipped to deliver the right kind of comfort or congratulations.

Want to really enjoy your child's development? Want to offer the right kind of support when they win or lose? Then be there for *the process*. That's how you earn the right to give advice. Once in a while, stick around and watch their practices. Talk about their goals in the car ride home. Volunteer to be an assistant coach. Watch videos and read how-to books. Anticipate what they need to do to succeed at the next level. Be honest with yourself. Do they have what it takes?

If your son or daughter chooses to rededicate themselves to pursue a dream, then help them go for it. Invest in the right coaching and the right professional-quality gear. Commit yourself to also having the right attitude. Don't push. Partner.

But if they thoughtfully decide God has something else in mind, that's even better. It takes courage to let a dream die and surrender to God's will.

When an era of a certain athletic, academic, or artistic pursuit comes to an end, it's difficult to acknowledge in the moment. But in the very near future, you and your young enthusiast will very likely look back and have no regrets. Even as you recall moments of frustration and loss, you will recognize the value of having done battle in the arena.

As Theodore Roosevelt said,

> It is not the critic who counts, not the man who points out how the strong man stumbled, or where the doer of deeds could have done better. The credit belongs to the man who is actually in the arena; whose face is marred by dust and sweat and blood; who strives valiantly; who errs, who comes up short again and again; who knows the great enthusiasms, the great devotions and spends himself in a worthy cause; who at the best, in the end, knows the triumph of high achievement, and who, at worst, if he fails, at least fails while daring greatly, knowing that his place shall never be among those cold and timid souls who know neither victory nor defeat.[1]

---

1. Excerpt from the speech "Citizenship in a Republic" delivered at the Sorbonne, in Paris, April 23, 1910.

When They Want Their Own Room

We lived on Weber Road for twelve years. When we moved in we had two kids. We moved out shortly after Rae Anne, number five, was born. For a while, her four brothers were in one bedroom. When we moved to Tyler Road, we added two more bedrooms and suddenly the bedtime rituals changed dramatically. For years I had been able to tuck in all my kids, read bedtime stories, and have great end-of-day conversations by visiting just one or two rooms.

With kids spread out in four rooms, our enchanting extended nighttime ritual that had meant so much for so long became almost impossible. To this day, that loss makes me sad. The older two boys and Rae Anne were looking forward to having their own rooms. But none of us realized what they would be giving up. Years later, the kids admitted they missed the many benefits of sharing a room that they had taken for granted. The brother-to-brother conversations. The tucking-in time with Dad. The security that comes from knowing there's someone else in the room to do battle with any monsters in the closet. Plus, sharing a confined space is excellent practice for later in life.

So take this as a warning, learned the hard way. Kids may insist they want their own room. But don't be in too much of a hurry to grant it. Even if there is an extra bedroom in the house, you may want to designate it as a guest room or office. You will be doing your kids a favor they don't even realize. And the mutually beneficial act of tucking in can go on for a few more years.

Lockbox for Scattered Stuff

A place for everything and everything in its place. That's the best way to run a shipshape house. Is there a cubby, drawer, closet, bin, shelf, cabinet, or basket for that toy, game, or sports gear? Then that's where it goes. Otherwise, it may be confiscated for a bit.

If Mom or Dad trip over it, then it goes in the lockbox. What's a lockbox? Any place you designate that kids don't have access to. A lockbox may or may not have an actual lock. How long is the confiscated item locked up? A day. A week. Or until some kind of repentance or compensation has been delivered.

I can hear the arguments now. "I wasn't done with it." "Joey left it out." "But you called us for dinner." "But I need those batting gloves for the game tomorrow."

They may have a valid argument. Those are issues you'll want to sort out judiciously. Sometimes a little grace is in order. Just make sure your kids know that an item is being released early because of *your* generous spirit, not because of *their* unnecessary whining. As a matter of fact, whining should probably lead to a longer incarceration of the item in question.

As stated above, a place for everything and everything in its place. Lesson learned.

Can We Talk?

For the most part, kids don't spend a lot of effort carving out times and places to have serious conversations with Mom or Dad. But when they do need to talk, we need to be ready. We also need to make it easy for them to ask.

It starts with not brushing off their silly questions when they're in early grammar school. "Where does the sun go at night?" "What happens to all the stairs at the bottom of the escalator?" "Where does poop go when you flush?" "What causes brain freeze when you drink a slushie too fast?"

Listen to their entire question. Ask a follow-up question. Feel free to laugh a little. Then explain as best you can. If you don't know the answer, please don't make something up. Your kids are smarter than you think, and they'll see right through you.

The real reason to give your full attention to little ones is that you want them to keep coming to you as they get older. The questions will become more difficult. But also more critical to their moral, educational, and spiritual development.

Sometime during those grade school years, see if the two of you can come up with a signal. One that allows your growing and inquisitive child to let you know an important dialogue is brewing. It could be as simple as "Hey, Mom, got a minute?" Or "Dad, can we have a catch?"

Dave and his daughter, Lauren, had a code. They liked sushi. Mom, not so much. So whenever either of them wanted to talk or just felt like going out, either one of them could say, "Hey, I feel like sushi," and they would head out on a daddy-daughter date—with Mom's blessing, of course.

In our home, the best conversations seemed to happen after dark, especially as kids got older. On dozens of occasions, one of our crew would knock on our master bedroom door and plop across the foot of our bed. After chitchatting about trivial matters for twenty minutes, they would reveal the real reason they were there by bringing up some issue that required input from Mom and Dad. That's one reason we eventually bought a king-size bed.

The point? Take a moment to consider each one of your kids. When they need to talk, do they each have a guaranteed pipeline with which to gain your full attention? Just as important, will you give it to them?

Hold Off on Dessert

At large family gatherings, especially Thanksgiving, the Payleitner family intentionally holds off dessert for an hour or so. And we talk. Most of the dirty dishes get cleared. Coffee gets poured. Sometimes we just catch up on family news. Sometimes, we get more intentional and pass around a basket with preprinted questions. *"What's your earliest memory?" "What are you most proud of this past year?" "What's the worst hairstyle you've ever had?" "What's the biggest challenge you're expecting in the next year?" "What nicknames have you been called?"* Maybe just one person answers each question. Maybe every person at the table gets a chance to reveal their memories, accomplishments, bad-hair days, hurdles, and nicknames. The conversation around the table swings from silly to serious.

The key is that everyone partakes. No one rushes off to do dishes, text girlfriends, or watch football. If a baby needs changing or someone has to excuse themselves to keep a commitment to their in-laws, that's perfectly fine. But for the most part, family members are glad to stay seated and share memories and dreams. It's satisfying. It's unifying. And, if you don't leave the table you get dessert . . . eventually!

Rites of Passage Bring New Rights and Responsibilities

Every parent knows that when a sixteen-year-old gets their driver's license, that provides your best chance to give a medium-length lecture on seat belts, speeding, car insurance, keeping the gas tank filled, and a reminder that cops are our friends.

Every parent also remembers the wonderful and encouraging conversations you had leading up to your child's first day of kindergarten. You didn't scare your five-year-old with terror-filled stories of mean teachers, bullies, lost backpacks, and punishment any time a student breaks a crayon. Instead, you got down at their level and told them with quiet enthusiasm about their very cool upcoming adventure.

Those are just two examples of turning points in the lives of our kids. During those elementary school years, other rites of passage include their first sleepover, first plane ride, first organized sports team, first piano lesson, first traveling sports team, and first camping trip. Plus, grown-up experiences like opening a bank account, pet-sitting, mowing the lawn, mowing the neighbor's lawn, setting their own alarm, and getting their first library card.

If you're not careful, many of these life "firsts" will slip by without notice. Especially if a child has older siblings, you may not even think twice about a first soccer game or pet-sitting job. But for each kid, it really is a big deal. And you should use these opportunities to speak new truths into their lives. Share memories. Give warnings. Set expectations. Maybe take photos and celebrate the event.

Then also, stay aware of turning points that are just between you and them, such as buying their first deodorant, bra, feminine hygiene product, and so on. Some rites of passage should be celebrated publicly and some not so much. Right?

Play Best Ball

Ompeting with your child is a good thing. It sharpens their skills and introduces them to new games, sports, and other skills. Kids don't mind losing to Mom or Dad. Kids of grade school age are even a bit disappointed when you're not very good at something.

For dads especially, you should dominate in checkers, driveway basketball, Ping-Pong, laser tag, trivia games, Monopoly, or Scrabble. You are expected to catch more fish, pull down more rebounds, or stack a higher house of cards. Go ahead and outperform them while you can. Just don't trash-talk or humiliate them. Be a model of good sportsmanship. Your domination will give the young competitor something to shoot for and a reason to keep asking you to play. Just don't forget to celebrate when they pass you by. Because, in the end, that's exactly what you want them to do. Right?

The one place where you can compete *while partnering* is on the golf course. Take your young golfer—maybe nine, ten, or eleven—to a par three course and play "best ball" or "scramble." That is, at the start of every hole both of you tee off. Decide who has the best lie, then both you and your golf prodigy each hit a shot from the same spot. During your early rounds, most of the time your shot will be used. But keep track of how many times your son or daughter has the better lie or makes the better shot. As you approach a green, you might find a bunker, while they fall short. They might make a five-foot putt you miss. Go back to the same course a few times each season, and don't be surprised if your total score goes down while your young golfer has more and more best balls. You both win.

The other benefits of a parent-child scramble is that you spend time *together* on the course, not zigzagging across the fairway and yelling at each other from fifty yards apart. Also, if a ball slices into the trees, feel free to let it go. That shot doesn't count anyway.

Fourteen Things

For sure, moms can do dad stuff. And dads can do mom stuff. But let's all agree that there are some things that tend to fall on one side of the fence or the other. What do you think?

Here are seven things dads are more likely to do: Skip rocks. Give horsey rides. Stop at historical markers. Play H-O-R-S-E. Give noogies. Tell knock-knock jokes. Carry a clean handkerchief.

Here are seven things moms are more likely to do: Kiss boo-boos. Know the location of the Scotch tape and the good scissors. Bake cupcakes. Shop for appropriate swimsuits that fit. Locate stuff in the refrigerator. Find a lost remote. And have Kleenex handy.

Are you nodding your head? Or shaking it in scorn? Are some of these fourteen items actually gender neutral? It's really okay if dads skip rocks and moms bake cupcakes, isn't it? We certainly shouldn't feel guilty for being ourselves.

No matter what, maybe the best use of these lists is admitting that boys and girls and moms and dads all have different tendencies and proficiencies. Also, let's affirm that when the head scratching and finger pointing is over, we're all in this together. We should probably all just go with our strengths.

Kids need to do kid stuff. Parents need to do parent stuff. And families need to do as much *together stuff* as possible.

Remember Grandma's Spin

Why do kids like grandmothers so much? You might think it's because Grandma spoils them, giving them everything they want. But actually that's not true at all. Somehow, grandmothers instinctively put a positive spin on everything. Which means it just *seems* like they are spoiling their grandkids. It's a trick you can learn and use to your advantage.

In a nutshell, instead of saying, "No dessert until you finish your broccoli," Grandma would say, "Finish your broccoli and we'll have dessert." The first is a stern warning, the second is an opportunity delivered with a smile. They both say the same thing.

Other examples:

"Pick up your toys and we'll put on Barney."

"Get that jacket zipped up and we'll go to the park."

"Finish that level on your video game and we'll go to the library."

"Stack those puzzles, put those Legos in the bin, and get all those books on the shelf because we need room to do that craft project I promised."

Notice there's not a negative word or raised voice anywhere in sight. You're using a carrot rather than a stick for motivation. Of course, sometimes that carrot takes a little effort and creativity. But you get the point. Positive spin beats negative nagging every time.

Why are grandmothers so good at this? Maybe they have fewer deadlines and less stress. Maybe they have more time, more patience, and more tempting desserts. The takeaway for moms and dads is—when you're attempting to motivate a stubborn kid—use the Grandma Spin to your best advantage.

Tide Sticks, Etc.

Typically, don't obsess about spills, wrinkles, frayed cuffs, or scuffed shoes. Family life is sometimes messy. Life goes on. But occasionally, kids need to be rescued from a minor clothing emergency. If you can instantly eliminate a small clothing calamity, then make that happen.

In the car or cupboard, keep a shoe box or pouch with a select group of very handy clothing repair items. Such as: Tide to Go Instant Stain Remover Pens (surprisingly, they really work), a lint brush, a small pair of scissors, needle and thread, safety pins of assorted sizes, and double-sided tape. Other popular brand-name items you may want to stock include Shoe Goo, Goo Gone, Kiwi Scuff Remover, Dryel On the Go, and Static Guard.

Beyond repairing wardrobe malfunctions, you may want to stock your emergency fashion bag with additional items, such as bobby pins, ChapStick, a black Sharpie, and a couple of earring backs. In our glove compartment, we even have a modest pair of spare earrings. More than once, on the way to an event, Rita has grabbed her earlobe and gasped, "I forgot earrings."

72

The 360

At some point during those grammar school years, the decision about what's on the walls of your children's bedroom transfers from Mom to the kids. Don't weep when the pinks, blues, and primary colors are painted or plastered over by posters and Fatheads. Don't be surprised when almost all of the stuffed animals, puzzles, and little-kid toys are tucked away, replaced by sports gear, art projects, tech gadgets, and sound systems. Your maturing child won't ever throw away the picture books you read to him over and over again, but those cherished memories will one day unexpectedly be boxed up and tucked away in a closet, attic, or basement. Mom, Dad, don't be alarmed. It's going to be okay.

So, how do you keep up with this child who lives in a room you don't recognize? You need to enter their world. Figuratively, that means going to their concerts, recitals, and games. Volunteering at their schools, clubs, teams, and church activities. Making sure your home is a welcoming and comfortable place to bring their friends. In a sense, you enter their world by proactively seeking opportunities to see what they do, who they hang out with, how they interact, and where they spend their time.

But you can also *literally* enter their world. The world they created for themselves just down the hallway. When the house is empty and you know there is zero chance that someone is going to walk in the front door, go ahead and walk into your child's revamped bedroom. Don't touch anything. Instead, just look. Do a 360-degree turn. Notice the world your child has constructed. Don't panic if you see a novel on the shelf about sexy vampires or a dystopian world order. Don't confiscate any PG-13 DVDs or CDs with labels that warn parents about explicit lyrics. Don't rip a poster off the wall because it features a boy band posing with ripped T-shirts and exposed abs. Also, don't start flipping through notebooks, journals, or diaries. If something is sitting out in the open, you can take a closer look. But the idea is to spend just three minutes in that room and then leave without a trace.

Make a mental note of your observations. Any areas of real concern might motivate you to keep your eyes and ears open. Again, don't panic. If you stop to consider all the temptations and corrupt values in today's world, you may realize that your son or daughter is actually doing pretty well. They're growing up and making new discoveries every day. They're sifting through their many options and making mostly good choices. If a decision takes an unpleasant turn, you're right there. That's the job you signed on for.

So do an occasional secret 360. Whatever you find, let it motivate you to redouble your efforts to stay involved in their lives. Plus, entering their world might help you gain new insight on future conversation topics, career guidance, vacation planning, and Christmas and birthday gifts.

73

Open-Door Policy

I f you discover your child is breaking rules behind a closed bedroom door, then set a new rule: Without express permission, the bedroom door will remain open.

If that rule is broken, take the door off the hinges. Make it clear that it will not be re-hung until their attitude is corrected and your trust is restored.

The Job Jar

One of the great advantages of modern technology is that parents finally have something to take away from their kids. When your grade schooler needs to be punished, you can say, "No screens for twenty-four hours," and that's a significant punishment. It's also convenient and effective. Just be careful you don't accidentally say, "No screens for a month" or "No screens for a year." Those are sanctions you won't be able to keep.

Used with care, cutting off screen time can be an excellent deterrent for future bad behavior. But who says punishments always have to be negative consequences? What if, instead of taking away a privilege, parents could actually benefit from the situation with a little extra help around the house? Wouldn't that be sweet? The problem is that when it's time to dole out a punishment, it's difficult to think of tasks that need doing on the spur of the moment.

What you need is a Job Jar. The Job Jar is an empty mayonnaise or pickle jar that contains dozens of slips of paper with household tasks that occasionally need doing. Jobs like vacuum first floor, unload dishwasher, clean litter box, pooper scoop the backyard, empty all the wastebaskets, clean window wells, dust living room, clean garage, sweep porch, scrub toilets, fold towels, read a book to a younger sibling, clean refrigerator, polish silver, fill a box for Goodwill, scrub bathtubs, wash car, polish shoes, clean sliding glass door, clean fish tank, wash dog, mow lawn, rake leaves, shovel sidewalk, Swiffer kitchen, polish woodwork, weed whack, outdoor litter pickup, scrub lawn chairs, shake throw rugs, clean bathroom mirrors, scrub garbage can, scrub recycling bin, and anything else you can think of.

When a child needs some course correction, you can tell them to pull one, two, or three tickets from the jar. Depending on the crime and the kid, you have the right to fine-tune, reevaluate, or overrule any job jar assignment. Maybe the job is not age appropriate or does not need attention on this particular day. In that case, simply have the culprit pick another slip.

Finally, you may want to include a few slips that say, "Grace. 1 Peter 4:8." If your young mischief-maker draws that slip, he or she is off the hook. Make it a teachable moment. Make sure to have the fortunate scoundrel look up that verse: "Above all, love each other deeply, because love covers over a multitude of sins."

The Answer Is 204

Ask "How many squares are on a checkerboard?" It's a great chance to teach kids the rhyme "Eight times eight fell on the floor. I picked it up, it was sixty-four." But, of course, if they say, "sixty-four," you'll want to point out there may be an even better answer. Then show how the entire checkerboard is a square. They may roll their eyes. Or they may say, "Okay, sixty-five." Then, of course, you ask, "Are there any other squares?" "Maybe squares that are two by two?" "Squares that are three by three?" "Four by four?" "Five by five?" "Six by six?" "Seven by seven?" The actual total is a whopping 204. And, yes, many of the squares are a little tricky to count because there are eight different sizes and they all overlap. Here's the math:

64 squares are 1x1.

49 squares are 2x2.

36 squares are 3x3.

25 squares are 4x4.

16 squares are 5x5.

9 squares are 6x6.

4 squares are 7x7.

1 square is 8x8.

With any brainteaser, the goal is never to make your kids feel stupid. The goal is to empower them to see how they can approach a challenging question from different angles. Explain that the answer sixty-four is not wrong. It's just that sometimes we should look beyond our first thought or perception. If we look at a problem or question from a few different angles, we may discover an even better answer.[1]

1. Portions excerpted from Jay Payleitner, *The Dad Book* (Eugene, OR: Harvest House, 2015), 35.

Keep Reading Out Loud

O f course you read picture books to your kids when they were toddlers. You cuddled them close, pointed to the pictures, made sound effects, used character voices, and led them to discover the morals of dozens of wonderful illustrated classics.

But what about after they can read for themselves? Is it silly to read out loud to a fourth grader? I say, keep reading. It's a gift to yourself *and* your kids.

Four or five nights a week, see if you can turn a few pages of a classic novel or short-story collection. I recommend *The Hobbit, The Chronicles of Narnia, The Phantom Tollbooth, Anne of Green Gables, Tom Sawyer, Charlotte's Web, Watership Down, The Voyages of Doctor Dolittle, Hans Christian Andersen's Fairy Tales, The Jungle Book, Old Yeller, The Gift of the Magi, The Velveteen Rabbit,* and *The Pilgrim's Progress.* Several years ago, William Bennett, former U.S. Secretary of Education, edited an anthology of short stories and poems, *The Book of Virtues,* which might be a good place to start.

Also, don't be afraid to crack the cover on more recent youth fiction. Be warned, the last couple of decades have produced novels for school-age kids that cover topics that can be controversial, such as divorce, racism, homosexuality, child abuse, bullying, suicide, and so on. These books do a reasonable job of bringing up the challenges of life in the twenty-first century. But they may not present values you support, which is another reason to keep reading. If a book—even a fictional story—features a character making unhealthy decisions or espousing moral judgments with which you don't agree, you don't necessarily have to stop reading. But you do need to be prepared and comfortable expressing your convictions.

Anytime you're reading—or even watching a television program with your kids—you should feel free to pause and thoughtfully say something like "It doesn't have to be that way" or "I know these are fictional characters, but I hope you see their choices are not really in line with God's plan." You can even toss in this idea: "Let's keep reading for a bit to see if the author has them face reasonable consequences for their actions."

Any time you can spend with your kids reading a book is golden. You're laying a foundation for their future that will serve them well. And last for generations.

Be Their Favorite Critic

Occasionally, your son or daughter may invite you to comment on something they have created. A song, short story, poem, sculpture, sketch, poster, painting, science project, business idea, comic strip, dance step, pastry, app idea, magic trick, robotic creation, hand-sewn garment, woodworking project, or crayon drawing. It could be something on which they spent minutes or months. In an instant, you might recognize genius or you may be wondering why your child is wasting your time with something so meaningless and poorly done. It may be their first attempt at a new genre or it may be a skill they've been polishing for years.

Your primary goal in that moment is to make sure they come back again next time they have something to show you. Said another way, they are counting on you to be honest, thoughtful, encouraging, and kind.

There are a variety of ways you could shut them down. Maybe forever. Judging too harshly. Not taking them seriously. Expecting too much too soon. Suggesting their time would be better spent elsewhere. Negatively comparing their work to others. Or—worst of all—dismissing their work too quickly.

The best response is to give them the gift of time. Whatever part of themselves they are revealing to you, don't rush to judgment. Take it in. Study it. Look at it from all sides. Ask them to show you again or explain some aspect of the choices they made. Ask for time to read the entire article, script, novel, or short story. Examine the fabric. Savor the taste. Listen to the *entire* song.

In middle school, after taking a few guitar lessons, I played a tune for my dad that was mostly just picking single notes. Before I finished, he interrupted, "When are you going to start strumming that thing?" A few years later, I asked him to read a short story I was working on. After a few paragraphs, he said, "Why don't you write about something you know about?" In later years, I only asked his opinion when I knew he would approve.

Mom and Dad, taking time in your assessments demonstrates that you are taking their efforts seriously. It gives you a chance to consider the impact of your words.

Your strategy might be to use the 80/20 rule. Only after delivering four encouraging comments, can you make one gentle suggestion. Finally, if you are critiquing the work of a young or beginning artist, writer, scientist, cook, or carpenter . . . be gentle. Err on the side of approval, positive feedback, and grace.

Start Cheap

Any time your kid expresses an interest in a new endeavor, express your own unequivocal support. It may be a musical instrument, a sport, a hobby, or an artistic pursuit. You can never really know how serious they are or how far they'll take it.

Squash their dream and you may be depriving the world of the next Rembrandt, Joshua Bell, Meryl Streep, Serena Williams, or Mickey Mantle. As a parent, your job is to give a word of encouragement, and even invest financially in their life experiment. But don't go overboard. Don't buy a million-dollar Stradivarius or $500 worth of oil paints and sable paintbrushes. Don't move to Hollywood and hire an acting coach. And please wait until they're in high school before buying an $800 Dunlop Max 200g Grand Slam racket.

Instead, start cheap. Give them a taste and see if they want and deserve more. You can buy a beginner's acoustic guitar for under a hundred bucks. Look for used pianos on Craigslist or your favorite online classified website. Sign them up for an inexpensive park district ballet class or children's theater class. Or don't even spend a nickel. Borrow some gear or equipment from a neighbor, an older cousin, or even your child's instructor. Most Little League teams have a good supply of aluminum bats for your beginning player to try.

Let your children know that if they commit to the quest and pursue it enthusiastically, you'll bankroll their efforts (within reason). If they don't take care of the equipment and supplies, or if they whine about practicing, then you can pull the plug and be relieved that you didn't invest an unnecessary fortune.

I witnessed my dad using this strategy with my eldest son. One Christmas, Papa bought Alec a cheap harmonica and said, "Play me a song and I'll buy you the best one in the store." Later that afternoon, Alec surprised us all by playing a snappy rendition of "Jingle Bells." Before the New Year, Papa took his grandson out for a pretty nice Hohner harmonica. Alec used that same instrument on stage more than a decade later.

More Than a Driveway

Allow me to inspire you with twenty-two things that happened on our driveway besides parking cars: A pig roast, a sidewalk chalk art gallery, intense four-square contests, amateur auto body shop repair, unicycle riding, Frisbee skipping, jump rope, Hula-Hoop, tandem bike maintenance, the classic Mentos-in-the-Diet-Coke trick, home run derby, homecoming pep rally practice, sun tea brewing, garage sales, skateboard/bike skiing, H-O-R-S-E, slam dunk contests, and dozens of games of stickball. One year, to celebrate their high school graduation, we crafted an eight-foot by twelve-foot mosaic of Isaac and his cousin Stephanie made entirely out of three-inch Post-it Notes and posted it on our garage door. Plus, of course, our driveway was home to lessons in starting a lawn mower, proper snow shoveling technique, and blacktop sealing the driveway itself.

How to Have Perfect Timing

When your kids are headed one direction with their attitude or temperament, sometimes you need a way to get them headed back in the other direction. What they were doing isn't necessarily terrible, but the timing, location, and circumstance are less than ideal.

For instance, they need to know they can't run down the hallway at Aunt Gert's nursing home. Also, it's not acceptable to wail like it's the end of the world when a dollar toy from the dollar store gets broken.

On the other hand, running up the driveway to hug Uncle Bill is a good thing. It's honorable to cry when the family dog gets put down. Timing is also important when it comes to sowing and reaping, and building and tearing down.

Even younger kids can understand that there is a time to be silent and patient. Other times, we may need to raise our voice in anger. And, yes, when our country's freedom is in danger, there can be a time to go to war.

Of course, we're talking about Ecclesiastes 3:1–8. It's a portion of Scripture that you'll want to read and discuss with your kids as part of a foundation of faith. I don't recommend you pull it out in a moment of disobedience or poor decision-making. Instead, read it with them *this week*. That will allow you time to read between the lines and talk about how it applies to so much of life. The passage confirms that God has perfect timing and he will make time for everything that needs to be done in our lives.

> There is a time for everything,
> and a season for every activity under the heavens:
> a time to be born and a time to die,
> a time to plant and a time to uproot,

a time to kill and a time to heal,
a time to tear down and a time to build,
a time to weep and a time to laugh,
a time to mourn and a time to dance,
a time to scatter stones and a time to gather them,
a time to embrace and a time to refrain from embracing,
a time to search and a time to give up,
a time to keep and a time to throw away,
a time to tear and a time to mend,
a time to be silent and a time to speak,
a time to love and a time to hate,
a time for war and a time for peace.

Help your kids really understand this passage and hide it in their hearts. When they start heading off in the wrong direction, you can give the brief reminder: "Son . . . daughter . . . this is not the time for that." They'll know what you mean, and they'll understand.

Mom and Dad, have you earned the right to say to your children, "Right now, this is a time we are going to gather, love, and listen"? I hope so. Just make sure you also leave plenty of time to laugh and dance and scatter stones.

About Your Secret Stash

Dear Parent,

Here on this page, tucked inside this helpful little book, is the official formal decree freeing you from all guilt for all time regarding your secret stash of Double Stuf Oreos, Girl Scout cookies, Fun Size candy bars, licorice, Peeps, M&Ms, or any other sweet or salty packaged food items you hide from your kids. Truthfully, you should be rewarded for rescuing them from the empty calories.

Please note: This guilt-removing decree does not apply to illegal, intoxicating, or homemade items. Illegal means illegal. Intoxicating is not something you should be hiding or keeping secret at all. Homemade should be shared before it spoils.

Finally, revealing the existence of your secret stash to your husband or wife is totally your call. I'm not a big fan of secrets between married couples. But this may be one of the few exceptions to that rule.

Low and Slow

Here are two words to remember when kids go off the deep end with whining, demanding, pouting, sassing, or tantruming. Especially in public. Repeat those two words to yourself, even as you take action.

Low. Get on their level. Eye to eye. Get quiet. See if you can shrink the entire episode down into a manageable, focused moment. I remember how Rita would get almost nose-to-nose with an unruly child with just enough room to put one finger up to gain their attention. Without speaking, that single pointer said two things. "Shhh! Don't say another word!" and "I've identified the problem in this situation and it's YOU."

Slow. After you get low, then speak deliberately. Be firm. Do not raise your voice. Whatever threat or promise you deliver, make sure you have the ability and courage to follow through. That includes taking away an iPad for twenty-four hours, earlier bedtime for one week, an extra chore, or a lost privilege.

If the meltdown happens in a department store or supermarket, you may need to exit the store immediately. You're not yanking them by the wrist while they scream their lungs out. You're exiting quietly and firmly.

No matter what, your low and slow response only works if you remain in control of your own emotions. In the end, the young attention-seeker got the attention he wanted. But it backfired on him. If you go low and slow, he will soon realize whining, pouting, sassing, and all the rest will not turn out like he'd hoped.

83

Teaching Centripetal Force

O n the next nice day, invite your second grader out to your driveway to wash your car. Ask him or her if they think you can spin a bucket of water over your head without spilling it. They will think you're joking. Then spin that bucket over your head without losing a drop. They'll be amazed, and you will have demonstrated centrifugal and centripetal force. (Look it up, if you don't remember.)

The best part about this trick is the dividends it pays in the next year or two at school. During some third or fourth grade physics lesson, the teacher will begin talking about centripetal force. One kid will already know all about it. Yours.

Suddenly your slightly above average child will be labeled a genius. That teacher and future teachers will expect a little more from your young scientist. Funny thing about expectations. They often tend to come true.

Armed With Science Trivia

Beyond centripetal force, there are thousands of scientific facts you can teach your kids—to impress them with your knowledge or set them up for success in school.

Consider the dozens of interesting and entertaining facts you already know. Think about your favorite high school subjects. Think about stuff you learned over the years watching the Discovery Channel or Animal Planet when you couldn't sleep at night.

Think about scientific concepts you learned the hard way in the course of life. Why bees sting. How mixing bleach with ammonia makes a toxic gas called chloramine. A standard household outlet delivers 120 volts, which is enough to throw a full-grown adult across a room. Goldfish can jump several inches over glass barriers. In subzero weather, soda cans left in a car trunk will expand and even explode. Isn't science wonderful?

Here are a few more facts that may make for an interesting conversation and learning experience.

The speed of light is 186,000 miles per second. By comparison, sound travels through air at about 760 miles per hour.

The call of the blue whale is louder than a jet engine.

Mercury is the only metal that is liquid at standard room temperature.

Think about the distance across a circle. If you multiply that distance by 3.14, you will have the distance around the circle. In other words, diameter times π equals circumference. In a geometry class, the formula would be written: $D \times \pi = C$.

Koalas sleep less than four hours every day.

There are 60,000 miles of blood vessels in the human body.

The wingspan of a Boeing 747 is longer than the Wright brothers' first flight, which lasted 12 seconds.

Of course, the Internet is filled with "facts." Some of which are not factual at all. That warning should be a regular part of any discussion about science. Just because it's posted, printed, written, or spoken doesn't make it true. Which is why one of the above seven "facts" is intentionally wrong. See if you and your youngster can figure out which one.

Volunteer for the Talent Show

While in fifth grade, Rae Anne came home pretty excited about the upcoming school talent show and informed me that a bunch of parents and kids would be performing together. And, by the way, she had already signed us up as a father–daughter act.

Well, since other parents were willing to embarrass themselves, who was I to weasel out? So after kicking around a few ideas, we decided to go with our strength—being wise guys. Rae Anne and I both appreciated wordplay, including parody, puns, knock-knock jokes, sarcasm, slapstick, and satire. And, of course, we loved baseball. So we settled on a complete word-for-word reenactment of the classic Abbott and Costello routine *Who's on First?*

We listened to a scratchy old recording of the bit and transcribed it word for word. Because of the repetition of the lines, the memorization wasn't easy. But we eventually had it down cold. To refresh your memory, here's a short excerpt. Rae Anne played the reporter. I played the coach.

Rae: That's what I want to find out. I want you to tell me the names of the fellows on the team.

Dad: I'm telling you. Who's on first, What's on second, I Don't Know is on third—

Rae: You know the fellows' names?

Dad: Yes.

Rae: Well, then, who's playing first?

Dad: Yes.

Rae: I mean the fellow's name on first base.

Dad: Who.

Rae: The fellow playin' first base.

Dad: Who.

Rae: The guy on first base.

Dad: Who is on first.

Rae: Well, what are you askin' me for?

Dad: I'm not asking you—I'm telling you. Who is on first.

Rae: I'm asking you—who's on first?

Dad: That's the man's name.

Rae: That's who's name?

Dad: Yes.

As you may or may not recall, the outfielders are Why, Because, and Nobody, the pitcher and catcher are Tomorrow and Today, and the short-stop is I Don't Give a Darn.

The afternoon of the talent show, the gym was packed with parents, staff, and every student in the school. There were some thirty acts. Rae and I were scheduled to perform number twenty or so.

As the first dozen acts unfolded, three things became very apparent. First, lots of kids in our town were taking piano lessons—some explored the keys impressively, while some could barely plink out "Twinkle, Twinkle, Little Star." Second, in 2003, there was no shame in lip-syncing to Britney Spears. I think we heard "Oops! I Did It Again" so many times that it was no longer ironic. And third, no other moms or dads were making an appearance on that stage.

I had been duped. Rae Anne insisted that other classmates had invited their parents' participation. Apparently those moms and dads were all smart enough to decline the offer.

The good news is that when our number came up, the crowd was eager for something completely different. And we gave it to them. Our comedic timing was impeccable. The laughs came early and often. We fluffed one or two lines, but no one seemed to notice. The applause was long and sincere. More than a decade later, I still get stopped in the grocery store by parents and teachers who remember our performance.

To be clear, this was not the beginning of a father-daughter act that toured the countryside. Thinking back, Rae Anne and I have not shared a stage since then. Really, it was simply a daughter asking a dad to do something fun and a little risky. And a dad who accepted the challenge and tried to make it special.

Rae and Jay were the highlight of the afternoon. And, I believe, all the other parents in the elementary school gym were just a little bit jealous.[1]

1. Portions excerpted from Jay Payleitner, *52 Things Daughters Need from Their Dads* (Eugene, OR: Harvest House, 2013), 115.

Identifying Potential
Without Adding Pressure

Your children were designed to do great things. God has a unique and surprising plan for each of them. Coming alongside your kids as they identify their purpose and sharpen their skills is one of the great rewards of parenting.

Regularly quote Ephesians 2:10 to your family: "For we are God's handiwork, created in Christ Jesus to do good works, which God prepared in advance for us to do." Let them know there's no panic or anguish involved as they seek to uncover God's plan. Instead, explain how it's one of the great adventures and privileges of life. Promise your support and partnership. But let them know it's their decision. Or more realistically, a series of decisions carried out over a lifetime.

Another great phrase to use is this: "You've got so many great gifts; I look forward to seeing how God will use those gifts to bring him glory."

One popular phrase you might want to avoid is "You can do anything you set your mind to." When he said those words, Benjamin Franklin may have been attempting to paraphrase the biblical passage "For I can do everything through Christ, who gives me strength" (Philippians 4:13 NLT). But old Ben may have been wrong. That verse shouldn't be interpreted as saying that every Christian can do everything imaginable. Read the passage in context and you'll see that Paul is revealing the secret of how to be content in all circumstances. That is, to depend on Christ for sustenance and strength.

So as you help your children discover their potential, make sure you send the message that it's not about how they are seen by their teachers, coaches, friends, pastors, or parents. It's about who they are in the eyes of their Creator. No pressure.

Getting Teachers on Your Side

My dad was a public school elementary principal for more than thirty years. He gave this advice to Rita and me when our kids started school: "Don't let your first interaction with a teacher or principal be a complaint."

In other words, early and often, be a bright spot in the day for your child's teachers. Not with gifts or bribes, but with your positive attitude and servant's heart. They're only human. They're building new relationships with dozens of families every year. And some parents are major hassles. Which means you will want to establish the reputation that you are on their side. Acknowledge their credentials and the monumental task they have. Care about them as individuals. Be a partner and resource for them. Volunteer, give words of encouragement, be optimistic, and send your kids to school well prepared and eager to learn.

In the course of a school year, you may need a favor or want to address a concern. Your son or daughter may need some special attention. Maybe you don't agree with a school policy or some teaching style. When you make an appointment with a teacher or principal, your reputation as an involved parent will have provided a much needed foundation for trust and a listening ear.

To put it bluntly, an angry parent with a zero positive track record will get zero empathy and little cooperation. Every school year only lasts until May. The reality is that educators know that if they can stall or delay the demands of a pushy parent for just a few months, the problem will very likely go away. When school resumes in the fall, if the conflict still exists, the burden has shifted to another teacher or school.

Parents, we need to acknowledge that during a typical school week, our children's teachers may very likely spend more time with our kids than we will. Engaging and supporting those influencers in a positive way is surely worth the effort. With that in mind, let's close this short chapter with a proverb that seems appropriate when it comes to dealing with teachers: "A word fitly spoken is like apples of gold in settings of silver" (Proverbs 25:11 NKJV).

The Bad-Apple Teachers

S orry, but if your son or daughter seems to have gotten stuck with a boring or lazy teacher, there's not much you can do. I don't recommend storming into the principal's office and insisting a change be made. You're setting yourself up for a battle you probably cannot win. Instead, double your efforts to stay involved in the school and classroom. You really never know; that teacher who seems stodgy or monotonous to you might be exactly what your child needs at this stage in their development.

On the other hand, there may be a way to increase the odds that, for example, your child gets the best fourth grade teacher in the building. It's not a sure thing. But first, you'll want to make sure you're proactively and positively involved in the life of your neighborhood school. Slowly but surely ease your way into a warm and welcoming relationship with the principal. In the final weeks of your child's third grade year, make an appointment. Talk with that principal about your great kid and ask which of the fourth grade teachers might be the best fit. Your message will be received.

Now, if there's something dangerous or evil going on in your child's classroom, that's another story. Get the facts. Recruit other level-headed parents. And stay calm as you approach the administration at the school and the superintendent's office. Once again, respectful diplomacy is the place to begin any battle with a school district.

Like All Your Kids Best

For most parents reading this book, the Smothers Brothers comedy duo was before your time. I bring it up because one of their punch lines resonates with quite a few kids—maybe yours.

Dick and Tommy Smothers would engage in snappy banter, and before long, Dick, the level-headed and logical brother, would get the upper hand. That's when Tommy would get quiet for a moment and say, "Oh, yeah. Well, Mom always liked you best."

It always got a laugh. But really, it's not funny at all.

I've recently become aware of several married couples who have two kids and they show a significant, noticeable preference for one child over the other. Now, I don't know all the specifics, but the entire concept makes my gut tighten and my teeth grind.

Apparently, in these households, the parents would intentionally choose to spend more time with one child and speak obvious words of discouragement to the other. Imagine any child—during his or her formative years—receiving a clear message that "My parents prefer my sibling to me." Or "My parents love my sibling more than me." That's near criminal.

I hope this idea repulses you as much as it does me. But I have to say, if you are recognizing yourself in the above paragraphs, take heed. Make sure every one of your kids feels loved, special, gifted, challenged, and destined for greatness. A parent's expectations and words of affirmation go a long way toward framing a future of achievement and helping a child reach his or her potential.

I have five kids. And believe me they have a wide range of gifts and abilities, continually surprising Rita and me with their accomplishments. Best of all, they cheer each other on in all their endeavors. If you're around me long enough, you will hear me brag about Alec, Randall, Max, Isaac, Rae Anne, and my four daughters-in-law. I honestly think I love them all equally.

But enough about my family. The questions to ask yourself are these: "Do my kids all know I love them without conditions?" "Do I pay sincere compliments and give authentic encouragement to all my kids?" "Have I helped each of my children explore their God-given gifts and talents and find a few things they're good at?" "Despite their differences, do my kids all get about the same amount of my personal attention?"

Dividing Your Time

It bears repeating. Thou shalt not play favorites among your kids. How to help your children discern and harvest their individual gifts is one of the great mysteries of parenting. It takes time. At certain crossroads and crunch times, one of your kids will need more of your attention than the others. The challenge is making sure that—over the long haul—you share your wisdom, time, financial investment, and love as equally as possible. It's not easy. They're all different.

One of your kids may gravitate toward sports, hobbies, and interests that have always been favorites for you. That's not a bad thing. But, you will want to intentionally become an expert in the interests of your other kids. (You may find some new hobbies!)

One of your kids may be a self-starter. Independent. A free spirit who doesn't seem to need you as much. (But they still do!)

One of your kids may be high maintenance. They exhaust you and drain your energy. Don't let them steal your time. But also don't avoid them. Find that middle ground.

One of your kids may have already checked out because they perceive themselves as second rate. Pull them back in! Build a bridge. Be their advocate and cheerleader.

Like so many parenting issues, just shining a light on the issue will help you come up with balanced solutions. A great way to do that is to talk about some of these issues openly as a family. Kids know what's going on. They talk. They see how busy life is. But they may not realize that family dynamics flow through different priorities. For a season, one kid may need more attention than his siblings.

In a series of discussions—or during one big family meeting—you can point out that finding a college for Frieda is going to be the focus of the next year. Or that Herbie is going through a tough time adjusting to middle school. Or, certainly, that we all need to pitch in and help with the newborn triplets. And maybe that's the best point. Parents should say right out loud, "We're all in this together."

Finally, if you are just now realizing that one of your kids has been neglected, go to them ASAP. Tell them you just came to this realization and apologize. Go overboard making it up to them. Spend time doing what they want to do for hours on end until they say something like "Mom . . . Dad . . . get a life." And then zing back with this beauty: "Sorry, dude. . . . Sorry, sweetie . . . you and the rest of this family *are* my life."

Explain 911

Sometime in the next few years, there's a very good chance one of your son's or daughter's goofball friends is going to make a prank 911 call and then hang up. Maybe from your house. Sorry, that's just what happens when your kids have goofball friends. Of course, virtually all 911 calls are instantly traced. Which means the 911 operator is going to call back. Don't worry. It *is* a criminal offense, but no one's going to jail. Still, your kid—and probably that knucklehead pal—need to know that what they did is not cool.

Here's an idea. Before that happens, explain 911. This week, give your kids a full breakdown of the 911 system—emphasizing that it is for emergencies only. Not a lost hamster. Not a big sister that's hogging the TV remote. But real emergencies, like a fire or when someone is passed out or bleeding badly. Or when an adult says, "Call 911!" When they punch those three buttons, almost immediately a helpful voice at the emergency dispatch center will say, "Nine-one-one, what's your emergency?" The system does have some flaws, such as difficulty pinpointing the exact location of cell phone calls, but overall it's well-designed and user-friendly. Kids also need to know that—like cops and firefighters—emergency operators are their friends.

Your instruction should include more than just how to push three buttons. Tell your kids to speak slowly and clearly and to listen to the operator. Tell them to explain what's going on and then give their location right away—the city, address, name of the building, what floor they're on, and so on. Especially if they're on a cell phone, they need to be ready to answer any question the operator may ask about location, or anything else.

Finally, if your child or a friend does accidentally dial 911, tell them to stay on the line and explain that it was a mistake. Otherwise, in most cases, the emergency operator will send someone out. That's especially not a good idea. Your kid's mistake could take the attention away from a real emergency. And no one wants that.

World Map Shower Curtain

Get your kids a globe. They'll spin it. They'll enjoy the pretty shapes and colors. Eventually they'll notice that—like a belt separating the hemispheres—the equator really does run through Ecuador as well as Colombia, Brazil, São Tomé and Principe, Gabon, Republic of the Congo, Democratic Republic of the Congo, Uganda, Kenya, Somalia, Maldives, Indonesia, and Kiribati. A total of thirteen countries and three oceans.

As your kids' curiosity grows, they'll notice that latitude lines are parallel, while longitude lines meet at the poles. Plus, they'll see that Greenland is not really as big as most flat maps seem to indicate. You may already know this, but when the spherical globe is translated to a large rectangle, the size relationship between countries is skewed. Countries further from the equator appear to cover more of an expanse than they actually do. The most dramatic example is Greenland. On the Mercator projection map, which was created by cartographers in 1569, Greenland looks like it covers about the same area as the entire continent of Africa. In truth, Africa is fourteen times larger than Greenland. More recent map projections give a more accurate representation of the true size relations between land masses.

While globes are quite useful, the best way to get your children aware of the location and proximity relationships between countries is to acquire a shower curtain featuring a map of the world. We did this almost by accident. Years ago, looking for a replacement shower curtain, we happened across a perfectly functional and relatively cheap model that kept the water in the tub and provided spontaneous hours of world map familiarity. Every shower was a geography lesson.

Kids need a reminder that a world exists beyond their own neighborhood. That's a great first step as they consider their own place in this world. For parents who want to take this conversation to the next level, may I suggest finding space on your walls for a full-size map or banner, provided by organizations like the Voice of the Martyrs, which highlights countries where Christians are imprisoned, persecuted, and even killed for their faith.

Finally, be aware that political boundaries and national identities change so frequently that any globe or map you buy—including this book—are probably already out-of-date. Thank goodness for the Internet. We know it's always accurate. :)

93

Barge Into Their World

Without asking permission from your almost teenager, sign up to help with a field trip, school dance, classroom party, church event, or fund raiser. Don't keep it a secret. Tell them soon after you make the commitment. Chances are they won't like it. Chances are they will try to get you to back out. If they ask sincerely and insistently, you may indeed want to respect their request and let the event coordinator know your plans have changed. But that's not the goal. You should do whatever it takes to get your maturing child to agree to your involvement.

Promise to be on your best behavior. Promise you won't talk to their friends. Promise you won't talk to *them* unless they talk first. Promise that you won't say, do, or wear anything embarrassing. And then follow through on those promises. We all know parents who don't know how to act their age. They wear clothes designed for teens and attempt to use all the latest jargon. Those parents inevitably fail on both attempts.

So be cool, Mom. Don't say something stupid, Dad. Stay in your assigned zone. Don't expect your child to hang out with you. When your child's friends come to say hi, don't interrogate them. The next day, don't analyze the event. Just be glad you had a chance to enter their world.

The goal is for you to fill your assigned role, have fun, and make your son or daughter glad you were there.

By the way, if the above plan backfires, you need to accept responsibility. But if it helps, you can blame your party crashing on this book you're reading.

Take Real Road Trips

I f time is precious, feel free to zoom through America on the interstate highways. Maybe you have one day to drive six hundred miles to Cousin Emily's wedding. Then twenty-four hours later, you have one day to drive home. Watch your speed. Drive carefully. And expect every member of the family to be exhausted Monday morning.

But if you're on vacation, I recommend you cover *less* ground and see *more* of America. Make it a priority to stop at historical markers, trading posts, greasy spoons, geological landmarks, mom-and-pop stores, and even the occasional tourist trap. That's what makes a vacation a vacation.

Get off the expressways. Memorable drives include the Seven Mile Bridge in the Florida Keys, still-existing segments of historic Route 66, and the cliff-hugging Pacific Coast Highway.

Get out of the car, stretch your legs, and keep your eyes open for the weird and the wonderful. The world's biggest ball of twine in Cawker City, Kansas. The Superman statue in Metropolis, Illinois. The concrete dinosaurs in Cabazon, California. Carhenge in Alliance, Nebraska.

Camping in the rain, blowing a gasket in the middle of Montana, bunking in a slightly creepy no-name motel, and getting pulled over by a cartoonish state trooper is exactly how memories are made.

By the way, insist your kids put down their screens for part of the trip. Unless, of course, they're searching the latest travel app for the next roadside attraction.

Please Don't Say "We'll See"

Kids are constantly coming up with wonderful things to do and places to go. Most of their ideas start with the same two words. "Can we go to Disney World this summer?" "Can we see the Grand Canyon?" "Can we go skiing this winter?"

In most cases, your instinct is to immediately reject the idea. You figure it's just easier to say no than to think through schedules, affordability, alternative options, practicality, and all that. Believe me, with five kids, I understand.

Perhaps worse than *no* is the unfortunate habit parents have of saying, "We'll see." You'll want to use those two words sparingly. Somewhere around third grade, kids learn those two words are the kiss of death. It's extremely frustrating for them. If you say no, their clever minds will begin to assemble and present arguments to change your mind. That's actually a fun challenge they're willing to take on. But if you say "We'll see," they know there's nothing they can do. They walk away disgruntled and defeated. If that's your goal, then congratulations. But that small victory is going to come back and bite you in the long run.

Here's an idea. When your creative and curious children express a sincere heartfelt desire, try to say yes. Or at least turn to face them, listen to their entire proposal, ask a few follow-up questions, and then say something like "Wow! That's a pretty interesting idea. It would take some planning, but let me think about it. I'll talk with your dad and we'll let you know!"

As you can see, that response is really just a slightly longer version of "We'll see." But it's a strategy that doesn't crush their little hearts. Plus, it leaves some hope on the table and actually may lead to a fun and rewarding future adventure for your family.

Making Bad Stuff Better

No one likes bad news. Especially when it's related to your kids. But when bad stuff happens, you want your kids to come to you. "Dad, I knocked over the birdbath." "Mom, I left the iPad outside overnight . . . in the rain." "Mom and Dad, you're going to get a call from Miss Crumwith about something that happened in the lunchroom today."

Your kids need to be confident that Dad and Mom will help make bad things better. There will still be consequences—maybe a significant punishment or some kind of restitution. They're not off the hook. But they know without a doubt that your attitude toward them will always be "I love you. It'll be okay. We'll get through this together." Say it out loud. Practice it. Use it often.

The three statements are undeniably true. You do love them. The bad stuff may sting for a while, but eventually it will be okay. And as a family you will get through this.

"I love you. It'll be okay. We'll get through this together" needs to be the attitude of your heart. When crud happens, your kids need to have those words hidden in their own hearts and minds. Establish that foundation for school-age kids when the stakes aren't quite so high. It will serve your family well when they enter the teenage years.

Believe it or not, you do want that phone call. "Dad, I wrecked the car." "Dad, I'm dropping out of school." "Dad, I'm in jail." "Dad, I'm pregnant." "Dad, my girlfriend is pregnant."

When life hits the fan, you want your kids coming to you, because the world does not love them. The world is broken. And the world will give them bad advice.[1]

---

1. Portions excerpted from Jay Payleitner, *The Dad Manifesto* (Eugene, OR: Harvest House, 2016), chapter 12.

Trusting Science

Explain to your young scholar that science sometimes gets it wrong. Said another way, over time—as scientists gain more information and develop new theories—they change their minds. Examples are many.

For decades, students were taught that Pluto was the ninth planet in our solar system. In 2006, poor Pluto was reclassified as a dwarf planet.

Until the 1980s, milk was recommended for treating ulcers. Doctors believed it coated your stomach and relieved symptoms, but they've since discovered milk can actually stimulate the production of stomach acid thereby aggravating the condition.

In the fourth century, Aristotle suggested that lower creatures, such as maggots, fleas, and tapeworms were the result of spontaneous generation. It was fifteen hundred years before Louis Pasteur put an end to such nonsense.

In 1870, a German chemist misplaced a decimal point when he was measuring the amount of iron found in spinach. For decades, nutritionists believed spinach had superlative muscle building capacity. It doesn't. But that's the reason cartoonist Bud Agendorf had Popeye eat can after can of the mushy green veggie.

Also, of course, the earth is not the center of the universe, toads don't give you warts, bats are not blind, and an apple a day probably does not keep any doctors away. Science evolves.

To be sure, biology, chemistry, physics, agronomy, archaeology, astronomy, genetics, meteorology, and just about every branch of science have done great things for humankind. Science should not be dismissed or mocked. The sincere pursuit of truth is always worthwhile. And, by the way, the pursuit of truth will always eventually lead to God. And our kids need to know that.

God is truth. Scripture is truth. Jeremiah 29:13 quotes God: "You will seek me and find me when you seek me with all your heart." So never fear science. But take all human discoveries with a healthy understanding that people make mistakes. Something presented as indisputable fact from a reliable source of well-intentioned human scientists may one day be proven wrong.

Only God gets it right 100 percent of the time. He never changes. What he does and what he provides is perfect. James 1:17 promises: "Every good and perfect gift is from above, coming down from the Father of the heavenly lights, who does not change like shifting shadows." You and your kids can count on it.

Make Your Kids Your Hobby

I applaud any and all of your hobbies. Scrapbooking. Gaming. Genealogy. Crafting. Golf. Tennis. Softball. Squash. Jogging. Bowling. Horseback riding. Spelunking. Coloring. Podcasting. Blogging. Book club. Movies. Working out. Photography. Traveling. Gardening. Such activities make you a more interesting person and a better parent.

But, for a season of life, *make your kids your hobby*. Set aside your own avocations and private passions. Joyfully give every extra moment you have to those kids you love so much. Maybe even temporarily suspend your involvement in any activity that distracts from your parenting role.

Does that sound radical? Maybe. But I promise the time you invest in your kids will not be wasted. The cliché is not at all cliché. *They grow up so fast.* That snot-nosed curtain-climber who makes you want to pull your hair out will be all grown up and out the door before you know it. Yes, I understand that sometimes a single day with your needy kids can drag on forever. But I promise that someday, when you look back, it will be one giant blur.

How do you make your kids your hobby? Look at them as a puzzle. What are their interests? How can you nurture their gifts? Look at your community. Where might they fit? How can they try new things while you cheer them on? Look at their world. Can you coach their teams or volunteer in their classroom? Where might they blossom or flourish?

Don't make it an obsession. It's merely a concept that helps you prioritize this season of your life. Make. Your kids. Your hobby. Sounds like fun, doesn't it?

Introduce Your Hobby to Your Kids

I f you prefer, you can ignore that last chapter. As a matter of fact, quite a few of you bristled at the thought of giving up your one chance per week to escape your needy kids and do something for yourself.

That's actually a pretty good instinct. An evening with other adults playing softball, quilting, or playing bunco might be the perfect way for a frazzled mom or dad to recharge and de-stress. Solo hours spent on a bridle path, with a paintbrush, at a keyboard, or in a darkroom may provide a valuable opportunity to think about what's really important and even spend quality time with God.

So keep at it. Pursue your leisure pastime with excellence—without guilt. Then, at the right time, invite your kids into that world. Teach your son about the care and pruning of roses. Play a round of golf with your daughter. Ask their opinions of your blog or podcast. Reveal the secrets of cabinetmaking or needlepoint. Show them where they fit in the family tree and introduce them to their great-great-great grandfather. With one or all of your kids, explore a cave, ride horses, or go to an art film. Or partner with them on a quest to find the perfect addition to your growing antique collection.

By inviting them into your world, there's a better chance they will invite you into theirs. Plus, there's also the chance that one of your offspring will be totally enchanted with your hobby. Which means you'll have fascinating conversations and shared secrets with your son or daughter for decades to come.

Kiss Your Spouse in the Kitchen

With marriages breaking up all around them, your kids need to know that Mom and Dad are committed to each other and that marriage works.

So I recommend the kitchen make out. It achieves three worthy objectives. It confirms the love you and your spouse have for each other. It tells your kids their parents' marriage is secure. It demonstrates that passion can still exist within a committed, lifelong marriage relationship.

Most kisses your kids see on television are between couples that are not married. (At least not to each other.) Hollywood seems to think that after the wedding ceremony, the romance is gone. Well, I disagree. And so does God. Ecclesiastes 9:9 even confirms, "Enjoy life with your wife, whom you love."

So kiss your bride in the kitchen. The goal is for your fourth grader to go, "Ewww!" or your teenager to wisecrack, "Get a room!" That's a sure signal you're doing it right.[1]

---

1. Portions excerpted from Payleitner, *The Dad Manifesto*, chapter 29.

Sometimes Say No

When you say no to your kids, you're in good company. As recorded in Scripture, Jesus says no more than a few times.

Jesus says no to Satan during forty days of fasting in the desert before beginning his earthly ministry. Satan tells Jesus to satisfy his hunger simply by turning stones into bread. Jesus says no because his purpose over the next few years is much greater than Satan can imagine (Matthew 4:1–11).

Jesus visits the home of two sisters, and Martha is ticked that she is stuck with all the food preparation. Martha asks Jesus to insist her sister help in the kitchen: "Tell her to help me!" Jesus says no and affirms, "Mary has chosen what is better" (Luke 10:38–42).

One day, on the road to Jerusalem, a potential new follower asks for a few days to say good-bye to his family. Jesus says no, confirming that once you choose him, there's no turning back (Luke 9:61–62).

In his hometown of Nazareth, the people are amazed by Jesus' teachings, but they still can't get over the idea that he is just a local carpenter. They are offended by his claims. Jesus heals a few people there, but because he is dishonored, he says no to doing other miracles (Mark 6:1–6).

After watching Jesus being betrayed with a kiss by Judas, Peter angrily cuts off the ear of the high priest's servant. Knowing that the events of the next few days are the turning point for the future of humankind, Jesus tells Peter no: "Put your sword away! Shall I not drink the cup the Father has given me?" (John 18:1–11).

Mom and Dad, it really is wise and healthy to say no to your kids. It's good practice for them. They need to know they can't always get what they want here on earth. And sometimes no is the right thing to say. They need to say no to temptation and no to kids who want them to do things they know are wrong. They need to say no to distractions that keep them from Jesus. They need to say no when God is dishonored. They need to say no when God's plan is being threatened.

Stop Yelling at Referees

Being a jerk in the stands has long been one of my downfalls. To be clear, I never yelled at the young athletes, mostly at refs and umpires. Frustration boiled over. I thought somehow I could influence their decisions. (I couldn't.)

I've improved over the years, but I still look back with regret, knowing that I probably looked really foolish and sometimes embarrassed my kids. Maybe some of the coping strategies I learned the hard way will work for you. I offer them for all parents, because this is not just a "dad thing." I've seen moms in the bleachers go temporarily insane too.

- Give your spouse permission to say something when this happens or is about to happen. Even before the game, ask for her prayers and maybe even talk over some signals she could use to remind you that you're starting to go overboard.

- Remove yourself from the action. Walk down to the end zone or foul pole. Find an empty spot in the bleachers. Distance sometimes helps. Often it's the reaction of the other fans that seems to stir the enthusiasm. Getting away from the crowd reduces the zeal and reduces the decibels of your cheers and/or jeers.

- Give yourself a physical reminder of your promise to hold your tongue. Hold your car keys in your hand to remind yourself to think twice before any outburst. Sharply dig them into your palm if you need to. I've used that strategy at middle school basketball games.

- Distract yourself with game-day responsibilities. Volunteer to keep score, shoot game video, work the concession stand, work the chain gang, or be the ref yourself!

Take it from someone who's been there. You will want to get your jerk-in-the-stands habit under control before you embarrass yourself and your family, and before you do irreparable damage to your relationship with your son or daughter.

Turning Negatives to Positives

Do your kids engage in some negative behavior you'd like to see change? Silly question, right? Of course they do.

Well, instead of nagging, begging, ignoring, or surrendering your authority, do the exact opposite. Do a quick analysis of their behavior and see if you can come up with a plan that turns a frustration into a victory.

- Want them to put down the video game? Toss them a fresh can of tennis balls and send them to the park district courts. (Or join them!)
- Want them to eat vegetables? Serve veggies they like. Let them pick out interesting new fresh veggies at the store. Ask for their help finding new recipes.
- Want them to stop smoking pot? Take them mountain biking. Or hang gliding. Or find some other high they can get naturally. (With you.)
- Do they complain about what's for dinner? Sign them up to volunteer with you at a soup kitchen.
- Want them to go to bed when they're told? Start a chapter book that leaves kids wanting more. Closing the book after one or two exciting chapters will make them eager for bed tomorrow night.

Do you see how flipping the problem leads to the payoff? You're not just nagging your kids to stop an activity. You're turning a negative into a positive. Hey, if it works for their negative behavior, try it on your own bad habits.

- Want to stop smoking? Say yes to celery, whiter teeth, and fresh-smelling drapes.

- Want to cut down on desserts? Take a walk after dinner.

- Want to stop yelling at your kids for being late getting in the car for church Sunday mornings? Serve hot waffles one hour before the service begins.

- Want more attention from your spouse? Show a little more appreciation, respect, and affection.

This strategy calls to mind that great Old Testament passage: "Forget the former things; do not dwell on the past. See, I am doing a new thing! Now it springs up; do you not perceive it? I am making a way in the wilderness and streams in the wasteland" (Isaiah 43:18–19).

Kids Want to Work

Four-year-olds love to set the table, peel carrots, sweep the porch, and shovel snow. Right? So what happens between kindergarten and middle school?

Maybe adults take the joy out of work. We micromanage and disparage their finished product. We do jobs ourselves because it's faster with fewer mistakes. We don't take the time to instruct properly. Or maybe kids get the idea that work is nasty because they hear us grumbling about our bosses, co-workers, deadlines, low paychecks, and lack of job satisfaction.

It would be nice if we all could love every moment of our jobs, but that's not going to happen. At the very least, let's not drag every bit of baggage from work home with us. Let's set a tone and standard that says, "There's satisfaction in making an honest living and providing for your loved ones."

Kids really are initially excited about tackling a new task and seeing how they measure up. But their enthusiasm can be crushed when someone says, "You don't have to do that." Or worse, "Stop doing that because you're doing it wrong."

So, got a job to do around the house? Give it to the right child at the right age. If they have to stretch themselves a bit, that's great. You might even give them a wee bit more than they can handle, but not too much more. The goal is to limit their chances of failure and set them up for success.

The best choice is a job that has a beginning and end with something to show for their effort. Examples of what your kid might be able to do? Assemble a deck chair, seal coat the driveway, make waffles, make a salad, sweep the porch, collect the recyclables, change the baby, fold laundry, adjust all the clocks at Daylight Saving Time, turn the sprinkler on for one hour, stack the firewood, or paint the doghouse.

Avoid jobs that are impossible to track, like keeping the ice cube trays filled all summer long. Avoid jobs with high potential for severe criticism from Dad, like "Paint the front hallway." Avoid jobs with too much pressure, like "Proofread the speech I'm giving to the board of directors tomorrow."

The strategy is to supply them with clear goals, the right tools, just enough instruction, and then get out of their way. At the right intervals, you'll want to check in with them. Good questions to ask are "Any surprises?" "Got everything you need?" and "What's your schedule for the rest of the day?" If you put them in charge of a task, let them be in charge. Don't intervene, unless they ask for help. Also, don't be surprised if they're doing it a bit differently than you may expect. Let them try it their way. When they say the job is complete, don't nitpick. As much as possible, say things like "Nicely done." A day or two later, bring it up again. Thank them for their work. Admire some aspect of their achievement.

It's amusing to consider how putting your son or daughter in charge of a necessary task might play itself out. Assign a twelve-year-old the job of seal coating the driveway and they are going to push back a little. They may have watched you do it and know it's going to take some thought, time, and effort. They're also a little afraid of messing up. But your son or daughter will eventually take ownership. When the job is done, they may brag about it to their friends. And when some oil from Uncle Charlie's pickup drips on that fresh blacktop, watch out. Your child may express their extreme displeasure to their dear Uncle Charlie. That's a scene you won't want to miss.

When your child heads off into the real world, armed with a solid work ethic and the ability to finish a task, they will be rewarded with projects fit for a king. The Bible says, "Do you see someone skilled in their work? They will serve before kings" (Proverbs 22:29). Even better, they'll have you to thank.[1]

---

1. Excerpted from Payleitner, *10 Conversations Kids Need to Have with Their Dad*, 84–85.

Teach a Mad Skill

A mad skill is a mildly impressive or amusing ability that probably will *not* lead directly to large amounts of cash, scholarships, job offers, or world peace.

But more often than you might imagine, the implementation of a well-executed mad skill can break the ice in a tense situation, make someone smile, and even give your son or daughter just a bit more confidence and likability in their peer group.

What mad skill can you teach your son or daughter this week? Depending on their age and dexterity, consider:

Juggling

Whistling with your fingers

Reciting the alphabet backward

Naming all the presidents in twelve seconds

Hanging a spoon from your nose

Spinning a basketball on your index finger

Dollar bill origami

Nunchucks

Moonwalking

Back flips

Kip-ups

Harmonica

Drawing caricatures

Folding a really sweet airplane out of a single sheet of paper

Identifying key constellations: Big Dipper, Orion's Belt, the North Star

A few simple magic tricks

A few simple card tricks

Rubik's Cubing

Playing the spoons

Twisting balloon animals

If you know how to do any of these, you may be able to pass on the basics of your mad skill in a single afternoon. It's up to your child to follow through and practice. This list is not exhaustive; if you possess a mad skill not on this list, by all means pass it on.

Handing down mad skills yields multiple rewards. You impress your kids. You spend time with them. You equip them for success in the future. You watch—typically from a distance—as they utilize that mad skill. And, perhaps best of all, sometime after the fact they will think of you and smile.[1]

---

1. Portions excerpted from Jay Payleitner, *The Dad Book* (Eugene, OR: Harvest House, 2015), 92.

Peekaboo 2.0

emember playing peekaboo? Your tiny son or daughter didn't know where you went, but when you reappeared, they were glad to see you. Your big smile and bright eyes proved you were happy to see them. They laughed. You laughed. They laughed some more. Parenthood was one joyous moment after another. Remember?

So why did we stop? And what's the elementary school version of peekaboo?

We stopped because your baby's cognitive ability developed to a point where they were no longer wondering where you went and were no longer surprised by your reappearance. That's a good thing. It's called learning.

But is there a way we can bring that feeling back?

Let's do a quick inventory of the exact words that came out of your mouth during those peekaboo sessions from so long ago.

"I see you!"

"There you are!"

"There he is! There's my good guy."

"Hello, bright eyes!"

"There's my beautiful girl."

"Aaahhh . . . boo! Aaahhh . . . boo!"

You can probably add a few memorable phrases of your own. You had some great lines back then, didn't you? And remember the silly, squeaky voice you used? Are those memories making you smile?

Here's a thought. Not all, but most of those silly phrases—word for word—can still be used with your kids during this current season of life. Try a few of them right now. Skip the silly, squeaky voice. And probably don't use the word *Peekaboo*. But don't you think your fourth-grade daughter would respond to a warm smile and cheery greeting of "Hello, bright eyes!" or "There's my beautiful girl!"?

Like the first time you played, they may not know how to react. They may even be worried or frightened that you have gone off the deep end. It's all good. The smiles—and maybe even some laughter—will not be far behind.

Bring Their Night-Light

No one likes to wake up in a strange bed. In the dark. Especially in unfamiliar territory. Not even adults.

A familiar night-light can make all the difference. When your child is traveling—with or without you—pack the night-light from their own bedroom back home. (Or, one exactly like it.)

Your kid may be sleeping in the very next bed in a nice hotel room. Or at Grandma's house. Or in a sleeping bag on the floor of a friend's house at their first sleepover. Or in a slightly spooky cabin at a summer camp.

Don't make a big deal about it. You may want to check with whoever is in charge. But bringing a familiar night-light may be just the thing to turn the entire experience from a calamity to a cakewalk.

108

Answer Their Questions With Questions

Your child asks a question:

"At night, when there are no stars, where do they go?"

Now, you may not have even considered that concept since you were four years old, but with two seconds of thought you come up with your brilliant and accurate response.

"They are hidden by the clouds."

The question is answered. The child is satisfied. And you can get back to something much less important than talking with your curious kid. But what if you grabbed the moment as an opportunity to stir their little mind by answering their question with a question:

"Where do you think they are?"

If they hesitate, prompt them with additional questions.

"Are the stars still there?"
"How can something be there, if you can't see it?"
"Are your eyes open?"
"Is there something in the way?"
"What are stars, anyway?"
"What if a star was a lot closer? What would it look like?"
"Could the sun be a star?"

You see where this is going, right? Then, of course, you can always insert a silly question.

"What if all the stars just decided to play hide-and-seek?"
"What if it's God's birthday, and he blew out all the stars because he was pretending they were candles?"

As they get older, your questions can help your children dig deeper intellectually and soar higher spiritually.

"Where do the stars go during the day?"
"What's more important, the moon or the stars?"
"If you were lost, could you use the stars to help you get home?"
"How did the stars get there in the first place?"

This author did not make up this brilliant method of teaching. In scholarly circles, it's called the Socratic Method. I prefer to say we're following the example of Jesus, the greatest teacher of all time. The Bible documents more than 150 questions asked by Jesus, many of them in response to a question.

In Matthew, chapter 22, the Pharisees asked Jesus, "Is it right to pay the imperial tax to Caesar or not?" Jesus held up a denarius and replied, "Whose image is this? And whose inscription?"

In Luke 10, an expert in the law asks, "Teacher, what must I do to inherit eternal life?" Jesus replied, "What is written in the Law? How do you read it?"

In Mark 8, his disciples answered, "But where in this remote place can anyone get enough bread to feed them?" Jesus asked, "How many loaves do you have?"

So next time your kid comes to you with a question, ask yourself, "What would Jesus ask?"[1]

---

1. Adapted from Payleitner, *52 Things Kids Need From a Dad* (Eugene, OR: Harvest House, 2010), 45–47.

109

Ice Pucks

nstead of slapping around a hard rubber disk on a slick icy surface, how about slapping around a slick icy disc on a hard dry surface?

If you have a young hockey enthusiast in the house, this summer surprise them with a batch of regulation size hockey pucks made of ice. No recipe needed. Just put an inch and a half of water in a few good-sized coffee mugs or round Tupperware containers and freeze. Your gift of three or four ice pucks may be met initially with a confused look, but that's half the fun. When they realize you've created an entire new version of street hockey, you'll be hero for at least a day. That's every parent's dream.

If ice pucks become a regular favorite in your driveway, send me a pic of your son or daughter in full gear.

110

Who Here Has...?

With most extended families, it's not easy to get large groups together. It's even more difficult to connect generations.

We're all pulled in too many different directions. Holidays are overcommitted. Summers are jammed. Sports seasons overlap. Typically, it takes a wedding or a funeral to draw a good crowd. But those events come with their own set of emotions and responsibilities.

When large families do gather, you want to make the most of it, with lots of interaction and connecting points. The challenge is that most generations seem to stick together with their own. Siblings in their 50s, 60s, and 70s may not see each other all that often, so they tend to catch up on old news. Cousins in their 30s and 40s compare notes and make judgments about raising kids and careers. That age group rarely wants advice from the over-the-hill crowd on either of those topics. The twenty-somethings and college-age young people are bragging and whining because that's what younger millennials do. If the school-age cousins and second cousins get along, they may be playing a game or getting into mostly harmless mischief. And, of course, Great grandma is off to the side trying to decipher who is saying what about whom.

For the most part, family reunions start out polite and respectful. Then one or two snide remarks leak out. Before long, feelings are hurt and sides are taken.

The problem is there are too many side conversations. I recommend that you try to gather the entire crowd in one area for some intentional memory sharing. Summon everyone to the largest room in the house, a banquet room, or a park pavilion. Appoint an energetic emcee and go through a list of questions. Ask for a show of hands and then probe for memorable stories. Everyone listens. Everyone wins.

Who here has worked in a restaurant?

Who here has served in the military?

Who here has been paid to play a sport?

Who here has been on TV?

Who here has sung on stage?

Who here has run a marathon?

Who here has dunked a basketball? Can you still?

Who here has bowled a 300 game?

Who here has seen the Grand Canyon? Times Square? The Florida Keys?

Who here has sold a piece of art?

Who here has started a business?

Who here has kicked a nasty habit?

Who here has spent a night in jail?

The goal is to give everyone a chance to share a memory and for younger family members to gain an appreciation for those who have gone before them. Of course, you can make up questions on the spot. Also, you'll want to customize questions for particular members of your audience. For example, if you know a family member present has competed in the Special Olympics, make sure they hear you ask, "Who here has won a medal for track?" If you know a paratrooper is in the circle, ask, "Who here has jumped out of an airplane?"

Finally, feel free to copy this entire list, add a few questions of your own, and hand out sheets so that every family member can follow along or even jot down their own memories worth sharing. It might even lead to some kind of published family history.

Stop Trying to Be On Time

For the first decade of family life, Jay and Rita Payleitner worked very hard to be on time. We would establish a firm departure time and hustle our one, two, three, four, or five kids into car seats and hit the road. If you know anything about buckling kids into car seats, you will not be surprised to hear we often arrived late.

Showing up fifteen minutes late at a family gathering or open house is typically no big deal. But it's a real problem with things that have specific starting times like sporting events and practices, church services, movies, Awana meetings, and school. We'd often end up sneaking in the back, missing the first few minutes, apologizing for our tardiness, and suffering minor, but unwelcome consequences.

That went on for years. Maybe we're slow learners. Maybe we just never took the time to consider another option. But at some point, Rita and I realized the goal should not be to be on time. The goal is *to be early*. I think it was one of our kids' hard-nosed coaches who said, "If you're not ten minutes early, you're late."

Suddenly life was better. It's amazing how much more enjoyable a journey and an event can be when you give yourself just a few extra minutes to get there. Speed limits are obeyed. Parking is easier. You get better seats. Kids are calmer. Yelling is reduced. And you no longer get judgmental looks from other attendees.

I can't say we're never late anymore. But quality of life improves dramatically when you give yourself just fifteen extra minutes. Try it.

The Amazing Sharpie

I f you have a small army of creative toddlers underfoot, do not leave Sharpies unguarded. You may have noticed that on every Sharpie, under the word *Sharpie,* are the words *Permanent Marker.* Take those words very seriously.

But you can also use that attribute to your advantage:

- Use a Sharpie on kids' party cups to identify whose drink is whose.

- Use Sharpies on Popsicle sticks in your garden to identify rows of planted seeds—without fading.

- Use a Sharpie on a prescription bottle—especially antibiotics that need to be used in a timely fashion and completely—to track when each dose is administered.

- On a baseball glove, write your child's last name and phone number. Not in embarrassingly huge letters and numbers, but just enough so that if it's lost or stolen, there's a reasonable chance you'll get it back.

- Color-code your kitchen calendar. Assign a color for each member of the family.

- Use Sharpies to label CDs without smearing.

- Find some of those cool flat stones that fit in the palm of your hand and write short, encouraging phrases or favorite emojis. "Be awesome today." "Carpe Diem." "Live Large." "Believe." "Emerson!" "Reese Rocks." (See what I did there?)

- A Sharpie in your purse or pocket comes in handy when you meet a celebrity and want their permanent autograph on just about anything!

Sharpie markers come in more than thirty colors, and most creative parents already know you can use them to dress up lampshades, sneakers, mugs, placemats, pillows, and so on.

An aside: There is a school of thought that suggests you should *not* put your child's first name on their backpacks, clothing, or lunchbox. A potential abductor might use that information to call out to a child and build a false sense of trust. Be wary. But also empower your kids to know just enough about "stranger danger" without making them fearful of exploring their world.

Finally, Sharpie tattoos . . . not recommended.

Laminate Stuff

I n this digital age, everything is saved in the "cloud." Nothing ever gets lost. You can find anything you want and print out a full-color copy anytime. Unless for some reason you can't. That's when you might want to take an extra step in the preservation process.

If your local newspaper runs a sweet little story with an accompanying photo of your kid working on some project or achieving some milestone, it will probably be available online. Go ahead and post it, tweet it, and send a link to everyone you know. But also, make sure you grab a *hard copy* of that newspaper, clip that article with a real pair of scissors, and preserve that clipping for future generations. I recommend you laminate it. Really.

These days, your child's name appears on all kinds of printed announcements, event programs, and team rosters. But there's still something special about "getting your name in the paper."

Your local office supply store has do-it-yourself kits for laminating clippings and one-of-a kind awards. Or drop off a few items and they'll do all the work of preserving those keepsakes for a couple of bucks. Often while you wait.

Don't go overboard. Typically, a file folder is the right place to archive most two-dimensional mementos like perfect attendance awards or concert programs. But an irreplaceable document that might fade or crumble with age just might deserve that extra attention.

Use the Classic Improv Rule

The Second City, the theater and school of improvisation founded in Chicago, is recognized around the world for churning out the most brilliant comedic minds of the last half century, and that's also where they developed the single most important rule of improv.

Alumni include Tina Fey, John Belushi, Harold Ramis, Bill Murray, Joan Rivers, John Candy, Bonnie Hunt, Tim Meadows, and Dan Aykroyd, among others. The two-word bedrock of all improvisation is "Yes, And."

That proven precept of improv wizardry makes sketches click and actors seem brilliant. Here's how it works: On stage, a performer makes a declarative statement. The task of the next performer is to affirm the statement and then add his or her own spin, allowing the scene to unfold and actors to ad lib without hesitation. For example, "Well, I must say the climb up here took longer than I anticipated." "For sure, but the view makes it all worthwhile." "It sure does. Don't get too close to the edge." "Don't worry about me; my backpack is equipped with parasailing wings." "Why, that's fantastic. Can you show me how they work?"

You can see how in just a few short lines, actors can craft an escalating scenario and even create some tension. The "Yes, And" rule only works if the performers trust and listen to each other. The same rule can apply when a child comes to a parent with an idea, problem, fear, or need.

"Dad, can we build a sandbox?" "That's a pretty good idea. Our backyard could use some more fun stuff."

"I don't know if I'll ever figure out long division." "Well, there are some math concepts that take longer to get than others. Where are you getting stuck?"

"At middle school, what if I can't get to my locker between classes?"
"Well, I guess you do have to get to class before the next bell rings. I'll bet we can find someone who knows how to work the system."

"Mom, I need $150 for a new Michael Kors purse." "Hmmm. He does make a nice shoulder bag. What are you carrying these days?"

"Yes, And" works as a parenting strategy because you're not necessarily *agreeing* to their demands or solving their problems, but you are *acknowledging* their needs and desires. The goal is to begin a dialogue that builds on their idea. First, demonstrate that you're on the same team. Then, you can steer the conversation in a way that allows you to apply your perspective, wisdom, and experience.

Next time you think about cutting off your children with a "No" or "Don't worry about it" or "In your dreams," instead give them your full attention, listen to what they have to say, acknowledge that you understand, and then add your own spin. And if that improv strategy doesn't work, try tap dancing.

Annual Photos

A classic online meme is the series of photos taken with the same people over several decades. There's the awkward father-son pose. The four sisters gaining attitude and wrinkles over forty years. The teacher who wore the same outfit every year for school pictures. These photos create compelling visual journeys through recent history. I recommend you begin one or two of your own sooner rather than later.

Intentionally or by accident, the Payleitner family did a few of those photographic journals.

When Alec was four months old, we posed him with a department store Santa. The next year, he cried while sitting on the same Santa's lap. We didn't exactly plan it, but posing with Santa became an annual tradition, and that little photo album became a fascinating chronicle of our growing family. In photos three, six, eight, and thirteen, another kid pops on to the scene. After the first two pages of the album, every Santa is different, but that only makes it more interesting. For some unknown reason, Alec just didn't want to sit on Santa's lap after he turned twenty-one, and that's where the photo album ends. And that's okay.

Another annual family photo occurred right after Easter brunch. In the restaurant courtyard, all seven of us, dressed in our spring holiday finery, lined up in order of height. Over the years, there was occasional debate as the order changed. I didn't mind moving from first to fourth. But when a younger brother passed up an older brother, a minor squabble may have ensued. The pictures tell the tale.

Tallest to shortest makes for a dramatic shot. We also used the same tactic when the eleven Payleitner cousins got together. There's a poolside shot I will always cherish of our kids and nieces, ages four to twenty, standing shoulder to shoulder.

Then there's my own personal epic fail regarding a planned annual photo. Five-year-old Rae Anne had found a best friend. Hannah, the smiley red-haired girl from down the block, was the perfect match for my feisty daughter. Neither was prissy or whiny or gossipy. They both had a competitive edge and weren't afraid to get dirty.

To celebrate their newfound friendship, I had Rae Anne and Hannah stand back-to-back on the corner of our backyard patio. I snapped a photo and promised to take the same photo in the same place every year until they graduated high school. They loved the idea and giggled at the thought of looking so far into the future.

That fall the little red-haired girl moved away. A thousand miles away.

Now, if the two girls really had been friends for a decade or more, we might have had to arrange for plane trips and coordinate vacation schedules and all that. But it turned out that Hannah was one of those summer friends that sweep in and out of your life. It's fun and wonderful. Then it's disappointing and painful.

To my five-year-old daughter, that photograph was tangible evidence of a tear-filled loss and Daddy's broken promise. But after a while, it became a blessing. With that photograph as a prop, Rita and I reminded Rae Anne that Hannah was moving to a new place with no friends at all. And that the best thing a true friend could do would be to pray for a wonderful, fabulous, awesome *new* friend for Hannah.

Trooper that she is, Rae Anne joined us as we prayed. And even added some surprising and thoughtful prayers of her own for Hannah's mom, dad, and brother.

Was it hard? Sure. Did it make it easier for Rae Anne to let go of her best friend? Not really. But it was the right thing to do. As I recall, at last report, Hannah was doing fine.

That entire episode from more than fifteen years ago has made me appreciate all my children's friends even more.

The story shouldn't be told without this addendum. That photo remains in a small collection of Rae Anne's precious memories. Once in a while, just to torment me, Rae will bring it to my attention and thank me sarcastically for taking that heartwarming and historic series of photos (totaling one) with her best friend Hannah.[1]

1. Portions excerpted from Jay Payleitner, *52 Ways to Pray for Your Kids* (Eugene, OR: Harvest House, 2015), 59–60.

116

Blind Spot Awareness

Form an alliance with your spouse pledging to notify each other whenever a car happens to be hanging out in your blind spot. Without hesitation or apology, the person riding shotgun should vocalize a warning to whoever is driving. The attitude needs to be helpful, matter-of-fact, and intentional.

It's actually a wise and possibly life-saving declaration. Even if the driver already knew about the other vehicle just behind in the next lane, he or she should express gratitude for the traffic tip.

"There's somebody in your blind spot."
"Got it, thanks."

Discuss this agreement with your spouse *before* your next road trip. Otherwise, the response from the driver will most likely be a non-gracious "I see it!" Which may be followed by teeth gritting and silence. Again, the goal is to empower the co-pilot—who is just trying to be helpful—to point out potential dangers, speed traps, or upcoming exits. Everybody wins.

Of course, there are many benefits to alerting each other about blind spots. That includes safer driving, an appreciation for the partnership of marriage, and modeling positive marital communication for the kids. Best of all, when the kids start driving, they'll be aware of the surprising way cars tend to hide in blind spots and they'll be willing to listen to your driving tips. Which are always helpful and always received graciously. Right?

Don't Toss That Refrigerator Box

orrugated cardboard is a beautiful thing. It's strong enough to stand on its own and support some weight. You can cut it, shape it, poke it, and paint it. When you're done, you feel no remorse tossing it in the recycling bin. How about some ideas on ways to use a big old cardboard box?

A refrigerator box can be unfolded to as much as sixteen feet. If you've got slightly daring kids of just the right age, that's the perfect length for a slide down your carpeted stairway. You may want to stack some sofa cushions at the bottom landing to minimize broken bones.

Cut a window in the box about three feet off the floor for an instant puppet theater. Have the kids decorate the cardboard or add a curtain. Use socks for puppets or have stuffed animals dance across the stage.

Gather a few more appliance boxes, add some duct or masking tape, and create a crawl-through maze. With a little imagination, appliances boxes can be shaped into train cars, automobiles, planes, rockets, time machines, elevators, forts, caves, castles, pirate ships, submarines, and, even, appliances. My genius friend Dave Wheeler sat in a cardboard box decorated like a computer and spent one afternoon accepting handwritten questions through one slot and dispensing clever answers from another slot.

Outdoors, a cardboard box can be used for target practice by pitchers, quarterbacks, soccer players, Frisbee golfers, rock throwers, or archers.

Finally, Mom and Dad, before you toss any giant cardboard box, see if there's any lawn furniture, rusty lamps, chipped end tables, or oversized craft projects that need to be spray-painted. Flat cardboard is a perfect disposable drop cloth.

On the Steps

Your child's bedroom should be a place of comfort, creativity, organization, and good cheer. It's a place they can focus on homework, think deep thoughts, dream big dreams, and feel secure enough to fall asleep at bedtime. It shouldn't be equated with penalties or castigation. The classic parenting punishment "Go to your room!" is not effective discipline.

What parents need is a punishment that removes a child from the family for a short period of time, allows them ample opportunity to consider their wrongdoing, keeps them within earshot so they can hear any fun they may be missing, and also keeps them close enough that you don't forget about them.

We successfully temporarily banished our children from the family with the words "On the steps!" Sending our kids to solitary confinement on the carpeted steps leading upstairs was the perfect consequence for minor violations, such as a moment of disrespect, an unnecessary lost temper, or an unprovoked altercation. The punishment would often last a mere ten minutes. It's amusing to recall how each kid responded differently. One might wail as if he were being sentenced to his own beheading, another would beg for forgiveness, not wanting to miss out on any family activity, one would grouse that true justice had been denied, and another would bounce over to the steps knowing he was getting what he deserved, and the exile wouldn't last very long at all. On the steps—with no gaming device, of course—they might pout, sing, sleep, yell out commentary, or stare at the ceiling.

It never lasted long. I suppose we could have set an alarm of some kind. Only a couple of times did we totally forget about the young criminal. It was always a useful punishment that had a beginning, middle, and end. Not too tough on the accused or the judge.

If you don't have carpeted steps, you can probably identify a chair or a corner. But there's something about that defined space and that clear command—"On the steps!"—that worked quite nicely for the Payleitner family.

Express Unconditional Love

Make sure your kids know there's nothing they can do that would cause you to withdraw your love. Also, they don't have to do anything to earn your love. Your love is based on who they are, not what they do.

Feel free to quote often from 1 Corinthians 13: "Love is patient, love is kind. It does not envy, it does not boast, it is not proud. It does not dishonor others, it is not self-seeking, it is not easily angered, it keeps no record of wrongs. Love does not delight in evil but rejoices with the truth. It always protects, always trusts, always hopes, always perseveres. Love never fails."

But before you teach your kids about love, you may want to do your own extended meditation on the topic. Mom and Dad, take the "love chapter" to heart. It's a pretty good checklist for parents. Be patient, be kind, be slow to anger, don't hang on to past mistakes, seek truth, protect, trust, hope, and persevere.

Your heartfelt desire for your kids to grow in those noble disciplines is the perfect motivation for you to practice them yourself.

No-Regret Parenting

A fter delivering a talk or doing an interview, I cannot count how many times I've heard some version of the comment *"I wish I'd had this information when my kids were younger."*

My response is usually "Well, start now! Even grown-up kids still need their parents." In many cases, I can also add, "And hey, grandkids will give you a second chance."

The truth is we shouldn't beat ourselves up. There are no perfect parents. We all mess up. The good news is that—for those who are called—God actually uses each and every experience in our lives to serve a greater purpose.

Still, the best parenting philosophy is to start young, be present, and be consistent. Pour instruction, guidance, and wisdom into your kids early and often. Proverbs 22:6 promises, "Start children off on the way they should go, and even when they are old they will not turn from it."

See if you agree with my interpretation of that passage. Before the age of ten or so, children are eager for your attention and experience. That's when parents have the best opportunity for establishing a foundation of faith, morality, and putting others first. As young people approach their teens, outside influences begin to have an increasing impact on their decisions. That includes friends, teachers, bosses, coaches, the media, entertainment, and so many other influencers who may not share your values. Your intentional involvement early and often will set your kids up for a life honoring to God.

Like much of Proverbs, that's a principle, not a guarantee. Kids with no guidance at an early age can still turn out awesome. Kids with fabulous parents can be led astray.

Mom and Dad, please don't allow parental regrets to paralyze your future parenting. You can start today. Your children at the age they are right now need your love, guidance, and correction. No matter what's going on, you can still move forward with love, patience, and a door that's always open. No regrets.

Exasperate Not

A pretty good verse for parents to memorize, needlepoint, or post on Pinterest is Ephesians 6:4: "Fathers, do not exasperate your children; instead, bring them up in the training and instruction of the Lord."

Read it a couple of times and then consider what kinds of things might exasperate your children. How about hypocrisy, unreasonable ultimatums, and ignoring their questions? According to Scripture, when you *don't* cause exasperation, you're on the right track. Your consistently conscientious actions—keeping your word, maintaining reasonable expectations, and listening to their questions and concerns—are the key to bringing them up in the training and instruction of the Lord.

Now, if your kid is just plain whiny, do what we did. We bought a charming wooden plaque that says *NO WHINING* and hung it above the door to the dining room. It worked great. For about twenty minutes.

Chess Strategies

Chess seems to be a lost art. If you know how to play, you owe it to future generations to make sure you teach your kids. As you know, the basic rules are fairly simple. You can teach your bright third grader in a single afternoon how each piece moves. They'll especially like pawn promotion. After a couple of games, you can teach them about castling, en passant, perpetual check, stalemate, and the fifty-move rule.

Don't force it. Chess isn't for everyone. But if they pick up on the game, make it your special connecting point for this season of life. Take their new interest as far as you want to. Encourage your young chess prodigy to join or start a chess club at school. A timing clock, travel chess set, or books on chess strategy can make great birthday or Christmas gifts. Teach your son or daughter how to record moves with official chess notation. Talk about chess etiquette like the touch-move rule and the no-talking rule. Explain how kibitzing, note-taking, and computer assist are expressly forbidden.

Like so many other pursuits, let their interest run its course. When they become grand masters, feel free to take some of the credit. If they move on to other endeavors after a few weeks, months, or years, don't feel bad at all. You've already given them a great gift. A bit of yourself.

Match Their Deposit

Will Rogers said, "The quickest way to double your money is to fold it in half and put it in your back pocket." That's pretty good advice. But for your kids, there may be an even better way.

When your children are eight or nine, walk with them into the big bank building downtown. Any reputable bank will do, but I'm picturing a lobby with marble walls, high ceilings, and pens chained to the counter. Without getting into the politics and economics of the American banking system, let's just say you want this to be an experience that builds confidence, not confusion or hesitation.

Have them bring along their life savings, gathered efficiently and counted accurately. Probably not in a piggy bank, but in an envelope or shoe box. That stash can include cash, maybe some coins, and any checks from Grandma. Then, open a savings account in your child's name.

Most established banks encourage savings accounts for young people, often set up in joint ownership with a parent and accruing no monthly service fees. It's typically not profitable for the bank, but it is good business. You'll want to call ahead to check on things like minimum balances and other possible stumbling blocks that might turn a positive transaction into one of those frustrating situations we've all experienced when dealing with tellers and loan officers.

Before you deposit every nickel of your son's or daughter's fortune, do two things. First, take out a small portion—maybe twenty bucks—and recommend they find a safe place in their room to keep it. While the money in the bank should be considered long-term savings, the twenty bucks is just in case they need something in the next few months. It's still being saved, but for a special occasion.

Second, whatever amount they deposit, match it. If they put in $63, you put in $63. If they put in $320, you put in $320. Let them know that as long as they keep saving, you'll match every dollar they deposit. Also let them know, it's *their* money now.

That relatively small investment just may launch them into a lifetime of savings and investing. If your kids are smart, they may keep hitting you up for matching funds with every bit of future income from baby-sitting, lawn mowing, and birthday gifts. When the time comes, there may be enough to buy a used car or fund a semester of college. In the back of their heads, they'll know that Mom and Dad helped build that little nest egg and that will guide them when the time comes to make their first withdrawal.

I heard a speaker once say that savings accounts aren't biblical, quoting Matthew 6:34, which says we should "not worry about tomorrow." But there's far more scriptural support for wise planning and setting aside part of our income for unexpected needs. Luke 14:28 suggests we plan ahead with any building project and "estimate the cost to see if you have enough money to complete it." Proverbs 13:11 says gathering "money little by little makes it grow." The parable of the talents in Matthew 25 confirms that money should be saved and invested wisely.

It's true—we don't know what tomorrow will bring. We also know that we shouldn't trust in money and we can't serve two masters. But for now, there's something oddly comforting when we can look at our U.S. currency and still read the words *In God We Trust*.

Avoiding Hypocrisy

T he last thing you want to be is the mom or dad who says, "Don't smoke," while you are lighting up. Or "Don't speed," while you adjust your radar detector. Also, don't be the guy calling yourself a devoted follower of Christ, and then cursing the rain as you head out the door hoping to play eighteen holes on a Sunday morning.

Smoking, speeding, swearing, and missing church are not the worst things in the world. But being hypocritical is heading down that unfortunate direction. The Bible takes a dim view of those who say one thing and do another.

> If you claim to be religious but don't control your tongue, you are fooling yourself, and your religion is worthless. (James 1:26 NLT)

> Whoever claims to love God yet hates a brother or sister is a liar. For whoever does not love their brother and sister, whom they have seen, cannot love God, whom they have not seen. (1 John 4:20)

> Why do you look at the speck of sawdust in your brother's eye and pay no attention to the plank in your own eye? How can you say to your brother, "Let me take the speck out of your eye," when all the time there is a plank in your own eye? You hypocrite, first take the plank out of your own eye, and then you will see clearly to remove the speck from your brother's eye. (Matthew 7:3–5)

As parents, avoiding hypocrisy is a two-part process. First, establish your values. Second, line up your heart, mind, words, and actions to match.

Now, if you aim low, you can live in the gutter and you never have to worry about being labeled a hypocrite. But that's not who you are and that's not what you want for your kids.

So—and this might be the toughest little chapter in this book—decide who you really want to be and what you really want to stand for. Aim high. Be rock solid. Commit to being the role model your kids need.

Following through may not be easy. But your conviction and effort mean you never have to wear the uncomfortable label of *hypocrite*. You may still mess up, but your commitment to high moral character means you will recognize your mistake and humbly ask forgiveness. That's something a hypocrite would never do.

Merge Calendars

You don't have to *do* everything on your kids' schedule, but you need to *know about* everything on their schedule.

Events generally fall into three categories. On top of the list is stuff parents should really try to attend. That includes concerts, recitals, games, matches, science fairs, PTO meetings, back-to-school nights, and parent-teacher conferences. Make these activities a priority. Don't beat yourself up if you just can't get there. However, if you promise your child you're gonna show, keep that promise. Otherwise, you've got some serious apologizing to do. Mom and Dad, your word should be gold.

The second kind of event on your children's calendars is stuff that's important to them, but you're not even invited to. Things like auditions, tryouts, standardized testing, sleepovers, classroom spelling bees, their best friend's birthday party, and so on.

Then there are things that are completely optional. Serving as a field trip chaperone or classroom helper. Taking them to the next blockbuster movie on the weekend it opens. (Or maybe a midnight showing.) Daddy-daughter dances at the park district. Storytelling time at the library. A baseball card show. An open gym. Ribbon-cutting at the new dance studio or Tae Kwon Do academy. These things come across your consciousness on community calendars, while talking with other parents, in the mail, at back-to-school nights, online, on bulletin boards, and while browsing the newspaper. If you don't put them on your calendar, you will never take advantage of them.

The reason to quite literally put your children's activities on your calendar is not to give you more things to do or to leave you feeling guilty for missing something. The goal is awareness and opportunity.

Being aware of what's going on in your child's life will help you have more meaningful and deeper conversations. Instead of asking, "How was your day?" you'll be able to say, "How was your field trip to the fire station?" Plus, seeing their events on your calendar will help you imagine their day and remind you to pray for them. Also, if you see several weeks in a row with only a few scheduled events, maybe it's time to expand your child's world with some new challenges.

Which brings us back to the idea of opportunities. When you look back on any given year, most of your days blend together, and most of your child's days blend together. But days when you intentionally spent time at an event *with* your son or daughter will stand out.

So whatever calendar you have—digital, on the fridge, on the wall, or some kind of At-A-Glance notebook—put your stuff and their stuff side by side. And then make the wisest of choices.

Ticket Stubs

Keep them all. Movies, concerts, theme parks, boarding passes, train tickets, museums, county fairs, Broadway shows, sporting events, sightseeing tours, conference name tags, and even funeral cards.

Drop those scraps of paper in a shadow box, giant glass jar, or shoe box. Compile them by date in a scrapbook alongside handwritten commentary. Pin them on a bulletin board. Or toss them in your sock drawer.

For some parents, keeping old tickets stubs are the closest they get to journaling. If you are so inclined, you can add a few words on the back of the ticket with a black or red sharpie, such as the names of those in attendance or one highlight of the event. The date is probably already on the ticket stub. The idea is to turn each ticket into an easy keepsake, not a burden. Just make sure you save it before it goes through the wash in your pants pocket.

Anytime you choose, sift through the stash and pull out one of those tickets or passes. See if you can remember details of the day. Who, what, when, where, how. Your grown-up distracted brain may not remember any specifics, but chances are your kids will!

Spiritual Gifts

f and when your child accepts Christ as Savior, he or she receives a gift or two or more from the Holy Spirit. These are user-friendly, valuable tools fully charged and ready to go.

Does that sound too good to be true? Actually, it's a sure thing. "There are different kinds of spiritual gifts, but the same Spirit is the source of them all. There are different kinds of service, but we serve the same Lord. God works in different ways, but it is the same God who does the work in all of us. A spiritual gift is given to each of us so we can help each other" (1 Corinthians 12:4–7 NLT).

Your child will need to identify and may need some practice to fully utilize its power, but his or her spiritual gift(s) are delivered and ready for the mission of helping reach others for Christ.

For your edification and discernment, here is a list of spiritual gifts gathered by Dr. Gene Wilkes, a respected author and pastor from Plano, Texas. These sixteen were taken from four different chapters in the New Testament: 1 Corinthians 12, Romans 12, Ephesians 4, and 1 Peter 4. They are leadership, administration, teaching, knowledge, wisdom, prophecy, discernment, exhortation, shepherding, faith, evangelism, apostleship, service/helps, mercy, giving, and hospitality. Other experts may add a few other spiritual gifts, and I encourage you to do your own research.

Without getting into too much more theology, here's the main truth parents need to remember about spiritual gifts. If children—even at a young age—understand the grip of sin and the power of grace, and freely accept the free gift of salvation through Christ, then they acquire this fire. They receive one or more of these spiritual gifts fully developed and ready to use. The only question is when, how, and if those gifts will be opened in service to the kingdom to give glory to God.

Vacation Driveway Checklist

A s you buckle in and head down the driveway, quickly and efficiently rattle off some version of this vacation checklist customized to your family:

Phones. Chargers. Wallets. Purses. Glasses. Prescriptions. Sunglasses. Laptops. Computer cords. Keys. Watches. Maps. Directions. Bibles. Books. Credit cards. Coupons. Shoes. Socks. Belts. Hanging clothes. Shaving kits. Sunscreen. Swimsuits. Towels. Hats. Gifts. Pillows. Blankets. Diaper bag. Girls' stuff. Deodorant. Shaving kits. Clean underwear. The "blue" bag. Munchies for the car.

The list varies depending on destination—beach vacations vs. out-of-town weddings vs. camping trips. If one of your kids needs a particular stuffed animal or blankie to fall asleep, that may be the most important item on the list. Once you start mentioning items that you can pick up cheap at any drugstore, you can stop talking.

The list also comes in handy when you leave hotels, cabins, and beach houses and head for home. Of course, make a final sweep of your lodging before checking out. If you do happen to find some precious necessity, you have my permission to slide that item into a cup holder or glove compartment. Fifty miles later, your son or daughter will suddenly shout, "We have to go back!" or "Oh crud!" That's when you innocently say, "Did you forget something?" When you produce the forgotten item, expect your child to be simultaneously relieved and angry at you. As a parent, you can take that heat because you know you're actually doing them a favor. They'll never forget that particular item again.[1]

---

1. Adapted from Jay Payleitner, *52 Things Kids Need From a Dad*, 105–106.

T-Shirt Quilts

At one point, my son Isaac counted a collection of more than 260 T-shirts. Some were souvenirs from vacations, including a Spiderman shirt from DisneyWorld. A few were from rock concerts, including the U2 Vertigo tour. There were probably close to a dozen Chicago Cubs shirts. Dozens more were from Isaac's own sports teams, class of 2006 events, park district programs, and other token participation awards from competitions, tournaments, and celebrations. Many were hand-me-downs from his three older brothers.

It also didn't help the growing pile of tees that over the years I had worked with four different clothing manufacturers, coming up with slogans for T-shirts. Things like "I don't tan, I rust," "Yes, I know I need a haircut," "Honorary Oompa Loompa," and "Only Three Bad Habits." For a Christian apparel company, I came up with lines like "Living for three-day weekends," which pointed to the verse "Christ died for our sins, just as the Scriptures said. He was buried, and he was raised from the dead on the third day" (1 Corinthians 15:3–4 NLT). A good stack of those tees made it into Isaac's collection.

The hero of this chapter is my bride, Rita, who took the most significant twenty T-shirts and turned them into a cherished quilt. Don't ask me how she did it. I do know there are Pinterest pages and websites devoted to these kinds of projects. Selecting which were the twenty "keepers" was not easy. But the process did include donating at least a hundred shirts to Goodwill.

If you're a seamstress or have a dear friend who does that kind of thing, go for it. Years later, your once highly involved child will cozy up under a quilt that brings back warm memories of his youth and reminds him of how much you care.

Don't Blindly Follow My Advice

L ots of logical parenting advice seems to be contradictory. Spend any time at all wading through the millions of pages and pointers that shovel out parenting insight and you'll quickly realize that you should never follow advice blindly. Examples?

"If you let your kids sleep in your bed they'll never learn to be independent."

"Never tell a kid you can't afford something because they'll fear your family is near bankruptcy."

"Let babies cry themselves out so they learn how to self-soothe."

"Offering to help a child when they get stuck on a problem will undermine their self-confidence."

"Never say 'great job' to a kid because that makes them too dependent on your affirmation."

There's a morsel of truth to all these statements, but I'm pretty sure it's okay for a kid to jump into bed with Mom and Dad during a thunderstorm or after a bad dream. Also, children need to know we cannot and should not buy everything we want. When a baby cries, pick her up. It's a beautiful thing when parents and kids work together to solve problems. Affirming words from a parent give confidence and courage.

So even though this brilliant book has brilliantly given you dozens of brilliant quick tips, it would be completely wrong to follow any of this advice without applying your own wise judgment and common sense. Although I could be wrong about that.

Say "I Miss You"

Maybe you're smack in the middle of that season when your kids are always around and always needing your attention. Parenting is constant. You fantasize about having two hours to yourself. Two hours to do nothing. Two hours to not answer another question or break up another fight or clean up another mess. If that's the case, make that break happen. Confirm your undying love to your spouse and then escape the madness by claiming two hours to yourself. Or maybe just dump the rugrats at Grandma's.

I get it. I understand. But I promise that sometime in the very near future, you are going to miss your kids.

Just when you are ready to pull your hair out, you will turn around and discover they have chosen to spend time someplace other than in the same room with you. It could be the basement, the backyard, or their bedroom. Maybe the house of a friend or neighbor. Maybe it's an after-school event or church outing.

At first, you won't feel abandoned. You'll experience a strange sense of freedom. Sure, there may be other kids or responsibilities that need your attention, but there's one fewer kid to deal with. It's kind of nice. For a while. And then you will start thinking about that kid. What's he doing? Who is she with? What is my beautiful, trusting child experiencing today without my complete protection and intervention to filter out the good from the bad?

You're not exactly worried about them. It's just that your world and their world have been all about coexisting in close proximity. Unexpectedly your two lives are better represented by one of those Venn diagrams with the overlapping circles. There's your life on one side and their life on the other, and you can only be sure of what's going on when your lives intersect.

You are literally spending less time together, which you notice a lot more than they do. They're testing new skills and exploring new options. Those are good things. With their busy lives, it's easy for kids to continue to the next stage of life as if everything is fine. And probably it is. Mom and Dad just need some assurance. Which means it's up to you to take the initiative.

Stop your growing child one day as they zoom past and say, "Hey, I miss you. Can I take you out for breakfast next week?" Or something like that. Then agree on a date and do everything possible to make it a pleasant event. Don't make it an inquisition or introduce a new set of boundaries. Try tossing out a few non-confrontational open-ended questions. Do more listening than talking.

Your maturing children's lives are only going to get busier. Taking a time-out now—just to slow down and catch up for a moment—will lay the groundwork for more coffee dates and midnight conversations in the years to come.

132

The Potty Mouth Log

ot a kid who curses and swears, insisting that it's not a big deal? "It's just words," he says. "People in movies and TV shows swear all the time, and so do all the kids at school."

In many ways, your kid is right. You're fighting against the current. Language has gotten coarser. We tend to accept more and more potty talk. But we're better than that, right? You want your kids to rise above the foulmouthed culture. So what's the best way to eliminate the use of words this author simply does not want to type here?

Get a notebook and have your child keep a log. On the cover write, "Foul language used by Eric." Using his name is critical. It gives him ownership of the contents of the notebook. Each time Eric drops a profanity in your presence, he is required to make note of the exact word, date, and time. Just like I didn't want to *type* those words, there's a good chance your son (or daughter) doesn't want to *write* those words.

At first your child might treat it like a game. Before long, the written evidence will be convicting and the desired goal—eliminating a few words from his vocabulary—is fairly easy to accomplish. The transformation may be quicker than you can imagine.

The last part of the challenge for parents is to encourage your son or daughter to stretch their new, more cordial language skills into other relationships. The Potty Mouth Log may get them to stop cursing or using vulgar slang in front of you. But they also need to realize language matters wherever they spend their time. Let them know it's hypocritical to act one way with friends and another way at home. Now that they've made an adult decision to stop smutty talk at home, they have the power to make the same decision with their friends and classmates. That's tougher to monitor, but it's a worthwhile conversation and reachable goal.[1]

1. Dr. Douglas A. Riley, *Dr. Riley's Box of Tricks: 80 Uncommon Solutions for Everyday Parenting Problems* (Philadelphia: Da Capo Press, 2011), 37.

133

S'mores

J ust a couple of years ago, for Father's Day, our son Max, who is a young dad himself, hauled a small load of bricks into our backyard and built a safe and sturdy fire pit. His creation replaced the rusty standing fire pit in which we had built dozens of small campfires since he was a boy.

Rita and I were thrilled and honored. His thoughtful gesture delivered several messages. First, Max was saying he appreciated the time spent around those campfires as a family. He also appreciated the time spent with his friends around those campfires after baseball practice, football games, and youth events. Rita and I had learned to give a small circle of teenagers their space, allowing them to talk, laugh, plan, and dream without adult interference. (Sometimes they invited us to join them!)

Max was also telling us that he wanted the tradition to continue. His growing family lives a mile and a half away, and he knows they will be invited regularly to enjoy a nice fire in my new brick fire pit.

There's also a multigenerational connection. My dad, who passed away a few years ago, had a small limestone fire pit in his sideyard. Max spent many evenings there with his four siblings, six cousins, and Papa.

All that to say, if your city code allows, put a fire pit in your backyard. With this writing, I pledge to always have a box of graham crackers, bag of marshmallows, and good supply of Hershey bars in a specific kitchen cabinet waiting for any one of my kids or grandkids to say, "Hey, Chief, can we start a fire?"

Saturday Morning Chores

See if you can introduce this concept early, so it becomes an expectation, not a burden. Make regular use of the phrase *Saturday morning chores*. During the week, go ahead and say things like "Let's not worry about that mess. We'll save it for Saturday morning chores." Or "It's Friday pizza night! Providing super fuel for Saturday morning chores!"

When Saturday morning comes, everyone knows that a bunch of stuff is going to get done before lunch. That's just the way life works. There's no agenda with SMC. We're not trying to trick kids into cleaning, straightening, weeding, mowing, sorting, tossing, sweeping, or vacuuming. It is what it is.

The benefits are obvious and numerous. SMC is a propitious start to the weekend. Fewer cartoons. Projects are tackled. Stuff gets accomplished as a family. During the week, you can reasonably put off a project without regrets. And, once in a while, you can surprise the family by taking a Saturday morning off!

Your kids might reasonably assume that every family has Saturday morning chores. Down the road, when they realize they've been working while their friends are goofing off, you can innocently say, "SMC is our family tradition I hope you'll use someday with your kids."

135

Buy an Art Easel

Not sure about your family, but we may have spent a bit too much money on athletic equipment and team fees for sports like soccer, baseball, and softball. Plus, some hitting lessons and a couple of trips to Cooperstown. Actually, it wasn't wasted. Other than my occasional embarrassing rants from the bleachers, I have no regrets.

I will not come up with a total amount of cash invested in my five kids' athletic careers. But I will say this: Maybe the best $110 we spent on non-school activities had nothing to do with sports. It was the spontaneous purchase of an art easel and some oil paints.

Mom and Dad, it's possible one of your kids has an artistic ability that that has gone undiscovered. In the early years of elementary school, you may get a glimmer. But for the most part, all second grade art projects look the same. In an effort to minimize discouragement, art teachers tend to have kids mimic an existing piece of artwork rather than create something original.

Then later—especially as they head into middle school or high school—it's possible that some kids may never get another chance to pick up a paintbrush, throw a pot, work in a darkroom, or weave a tapestry. Many sharp kids tend to focus on classes that more directly lead to jobs or scholarships. Or maybe they choose choir or band rather than the visual arts.

So here's what happened in our home. We bought those art supplies, set them up in a corner of the playroom, and didn't say much of anything. Eventually, three of our five kids began goofing around with them. The long-term result is a few drawings and pieces of art that hang on our walls today. And who really knows what other ways our kids and their kids may benefit from that comparatively low investment?

So buy an easel. It may lead to a glorious career or avocation in the arts for your son or daughter. The worst thing that can happen is they use it to play Pictionary, which helps develop an entirely different set of skills, leading one of your children to grow up to be a game-show host or motivational speaker.

136

Let Them Starve

The first time your precious little darling forgets his or her lunch—if you have time—jump in the car and drive it over to the school. When you drop it off at the school office, have a short chat with the school secretary. In the nicest possible way, let her know you don't expect to be making this trip again. Then ask what the school policy is for kids who have no lunch. You'll discover no child ever starved to death at your local elementary school. There may be an in-school lunch option that costs a buck or two. Most school cafeterias have a loaf of bread and some peanut butter for emergencies. Friends at your child's lunch table will share. Or maybe junior doesn't eat anything at all from 8 a.m. to 2:45 p.m.!

But again, the first time they forget, do your best to come to their rescue. After school that evening, let them know that your lunch delivery service is out of business for the rest of the year. You can even explain the options they have at school, if it ever happens again. (They will crinkle their nose at those options.)

At the same time, let your child know that you will fly to their assistance in any real emergency. That's what you signed up for as a parent. But in an effort to make your life and their life more productive, you are doing them a big favor by insisting they remember their own lunch.

Alternatives to Nagging

uestion: What's even worse than a whiny kid? Answer: A nagging mom or dad.

I dare you to replay in your head the last ten interactions with your children. Focus on those conversations in which you were attempting to persuade them to accomplish some task or cease some negative behavior. Now ask yourself: *How many of those dialogues or lectures included something that sounded like nagging coming out of my mouth?* Be honest. This self-analysis is just between you and yourself.

If you're not a nagger, move on to the next chapter. But if you are, please consider these two steps. First, ask yourself if your nagging strategy is working. If the answer is no, then move to step two, which is finding your own personal alternative to getting your point across.

Following are some non-nagging alternatives for occasions when things need to get done. Make lists. Leave sticky notes. Let some things slide. Hire someone else to do it. Hire someone else to do it and take the money out of your child's allowance. Give more clear-cut deadlines with very specific consequences. Ask kids to set their own deadlines. Send a sweet reminder text with a few carefully chosen smiley emojis. Have your spouse do the reminding for a change.

When it comes to controlling negative behavior, you may want to take the lead with your kids and agree on a "contract of repercussions." For example, if they leave wet towels on the floor, they will wash, dry, and fold a basket of family laundry. If they leave Coke cans in the family room, no soft drinks for a week. If they don't respond to your texts or phone calls, the phone is confiscated for three days. Make any and all repercussions relevant, short-term, and enforceable.

You can introduce the plan unilaterally without any fanfare. Or you can make a big deal about it by announcing, "Good news! I'm as sick of my nagging as you are. So I will never nag again. Instead . . ." and then explain your new alternative. At first your kids and spouse will be skeptical. They will think your plan is going to be more work for them. (And maybe it will be!) But soon, your entire family will fully appreciate the new non-nagging atmosphere. And so will you.

The Sarcastic Clap

The summer our four sons were between the ages of eighteen and twenty-six, they had a spur-of-the-moment idea to do a one-night camping excursion to a campground near Lake Geneva, Wisconsin. Not a big deal. Just the four of them. None were married yet. It was going to be one of those priceless brother-bonding experiences. And I was a little envious.

I asked Rita's opinion and she said it was okay, so I invited myself along. Without any hesitancy, all four boys said yes. I was grateful. Plus, it helped that I paid for gas, food, and campground fees.

Seeking solitude, we drove through the winding gravel roads to the furthest corner of the campground. We pitched our tent at the front edge of a dark, deep, dense woods. Or so we thought. As we sat around our campfire, we were surprised to hear voices coming from those woods. Pushing through the brush, we discovered that our tent was actually no more than forty yards from a paved road and across that road was a row of typical suburban-looking houses with driveways and front lawns. It turns out we weren't exactly wilderness camping. What's more, the voices we heard had a familiar cadence. It was a father instructing his nine- or ten-year-old son in running passing routes. My four young adult sons and I kept our distance, anticipating a flood of warm nostalgic memories of our own bonding moments tossing around a football.

Instead, the whole thing turned a bit creepy. The man would bark a command. The boy would sprint and make a cut while the father took a three-step drop as if he were Brett Favre, and fired a ball just out of reach or bouncing painfully off his son's chest. The father responded with only disparaging words, and the next throw was harder and more uncatchable!

Somehow, the boy eventually did catch one of those passes, and the father's response was the icing on the cake. The man did a painfully slow sarcastic clap, adding a word of fake encouragement to match, "Congratulations, you finally caught one."

Now, maybe that boy was a cocky know-it-all who needed a lesson in humility. Maybe we happened to catch that father on a tough night after a tough day. But I don't think so. The sarcasm came a bit too easy, and the son never responded with a laugh or a zinger of his own. I do hope that father and son worked things out, especially since that boy is probably off to college by now. Maybe on a football scholarship, but probably not.

Looking back, one good thing did come out of the evening the Payleitner men spied on that front-yard football practice. It was a gift received by *my* family—a lesson. And now I give that gift to you. Parents, please don't give sarcastic encouragement, and certainly don't use the sarcastic clap. Okay?

None of us will forget that night, especially since it's brought a touch of sardonic humor on occasion when Alec, Randall, Max, or Isaac toss around a football or Frisbee in our side yard. One of them may stop in the middle of the action and begin a pathetic slow applause for one of his brothers and satirically say, "Congratulations, you finally caught one."

The Cogent Power of Empathy

When their little heart is broken, be heartbroken with them. When they're worried about something coming up this weekend, be worried with them. When they're celebrating a victory, celebrate with them. When they're frustrated because something is happening over which they have no control, share their vexation.

Here's the point: When your child is experiencing an emotional moment, match that emotion. Later, you can add some insight, reminder, or warning. But for a while—maybe just a short period of time—your best course of action is not to fix or explain. Just be there.

If the gerbil dies, be sad. Sad can be good. Don't replace the gerbil right away.

If your daughter has butterflies in her tummy about her clarinet solo, go ahead and acknowledge that it's a big responsibility, adding that both you and her music teacher have great confidence in her.

If your son wins his division, enjoy the victory. There's no need to throw cold water on the moment by reminding him that his next opponent is even tougher. He already knows what's coming.

If some developer begins excavation on the empty field where they hang out with their friends, share their frustration. Maybe tell them about some experience from your own youth in which some business, school administration, or city council made a decision that took away something important to you.

Matching your children's emotions is an effective relationship tool. Romans 12:15 says, "Rejoice with those who rejoice; mourn with those who mourn." By acknowledging their emotions, your kids will be more likely to come to you and count on you whenever they have news—good or bad.

There's plenty of time later to put things in perspective and maybe even turn any of these emotional experiences into a teachable moment. But for a while, exhibit empathy. The world needs more empathy.

Ask for Their Help

There are things your six-year-old can do. Sometimes, even better than you. For example, crawl under the bed and retrieve a lost slipper. Run down to the basement to see if you left the light on in the workshop. Dig through the button box to find a button that matches another button. Quickly assemble toddler puzzles and stack them on the bookshelf. If you happen to be visiting their school, your youngster can answer "Which door should we go in?" In their bedroom, "What shelf does the box of crayons go on?" On the TV, "Which channel is Nickelodeon?" Six-year-olds like it when you ask for their help.

There are even more things a *ten*-year-old can do better than you. Especially as it relates to apps, social media, music downloads, television remotes, and other technology issues. (Which confirms you need to be ever-vigilant about what they're downloading, uploading, and experiencing.) Again, go ahead and ask for their help.

For the first ten years of life, children need to see their parents as nearly invincible and almost all-powerful. They want to know you can protect and provide for them. But that doesn't mean you can't use their help once in a while. Asking your kids for legitimately helpful help is empowering for both of you. They get to contribute. You get the assistance you need. Plus, you no longer have to give them fake assignments to make them feel like they're contributing. (Assignments like polishing door handles, holding screws, sanding wood scraps, and watching paint dry.)

I know asking for "help" from smaller children will typically slow you down. But getting them in the habit of helping may be one of the most important values you ever teach them. Your kids need to know they have gifts, they can contribute, they have value, and they are expected to do what they can when they can.

What's more, when they do step up to a task, they may very well be doing more than they think. Yes, they're learning a skill. Yes, they're contributing to the family. But they're also serving the Lord. Colossians 3:23–24 confirms, "Whatever you do, work at it with all your heart, as working for the Lord, not for human masters, since you know that you will receive an inheritance from the Lord as a reward. It is the Lord Christ you are serving."

Go Back to High School

When's the last time you were at a high school sporting event, theater production, band or choir concert, or art show? I've been to hundreds. But if all your kids are in elementary school, it may have been a decade or more since you've even set foot on a high school campus.

If you've moved away from your hometown, you probably have only driven past your local high school. When you think about your kids attending there in a few years, the building may even seem a bit intimidating. If that's true for you, think about how your kids might feel.

Here's an easy fix to that worry: Start taking your family to football games, musicals, and any other high school events that show up in your local newspaper. As a matter of fact, on any Saturday you can swing by and get free admission to sporting events of all kinds. A freshman girls' soccer game, a sophomore baseball game, lacrosse, and a track meet might all be going on at the same time. Varsity sports will charge admission. But underclass contests are typically free. Stop by and watch a couple of innings, a few races, or whatever.

Going back to high school is a powerful parenting hack. You're out with the kids. You're exposing them to activities they may want to consider in a few short years. You're becoming invested in the community. And you're making high school a place that's not scary at all.

Doing Life

My favorite piece of Scripture for parents is Deuteronomy 6:5–9. It really comes down to this thought: *Love God. And then pass that love on to your kids in the regular course of life.* Read it for yourself:

> Love the Lord your God with all your heart and with all your soul and with all your strength. These commandments that I give you today are to be on your hearts. Impress them on your children. Talk about them when you sit at home and when you walk along the road, when you lie down and when you get up. Tie them as symbols on your hands and bind them on your foreheads. Write them on the doorframes of your houses and on your gates.

There are all kinds of historical and theological references in that passage, but here's how I read it: Moms and Dads, put God first. Know, love, and trust him. And then invite your kids into that same relationship. Don't put God in a box. Talk about how God is constantly working in our lives. Have those intentional conversations anytime and all the time. Watching TV. Strolling down a dirt road. Tucking in. Chatting over waffles. God's impact in our lives should be reflected in all we do and evident to everyone we meet.

Be Happy to See Them

magine your child *not in your presence* for a certain length of time. An hour doing homework upstairs, an afternoon at a friend's house, at school for the day, at church camp for a weekend, at college for a semester, or three years in Europe.

When you see them next, *will their presence bring you joy?* I hope so.

Now consider the situation from their perspective. *Will they be happy to see you?* Interesting question, isn't it?

Here's your assignment. Now and forever. Do whatever it takes for your children to be happy to see you.

Even if you had a cruddy day. Even if they're a half hour past curfew. Even if their room is a pigsty and they forgot to feed the goldfish—all of whom are now floating upside down in the bowl. Even if you have to fake it.

Here's a hint: The best way to ensure that your son or daughter will be happy to see you . . . is for you to be happy to see them.

See the Seasons

So, what season are you in?

Newly pregnant. Birthing classes. False labor. Nesting. APGAR score. Counting fingers and toes. Phone call to grandparents. Way-too-short hospital stay. Car seat frustrations. Two a.m. feedings. Colic. Swaddling. Lullabies. Bouncy seats. Finally sleeping through the night! Changing tables. Spitting up. Running out of diapers. Frantically checking developmental charts. Rolling over. Baby-proofing outlets. Crawling. Rolling a ball. Crawling fast. Banging pots and pans. Standing. Teetering. Walking, falling, walking. Earaches. Stinky diapers. Really stinky diapers. Gurgling. Talking. Spitting. Biting. Burbling those warm, red cheeks. The not-so-terrible twos. Wagons. Mimicking. Running. Board books. Sentences. Tricycles. Singing. Scribbling. Lots of hugs and kisses. Bedtime stories. Dancing. Cousins. Friends. Drawing pictures of the family. Playdates. Keyboards. Nursery school. New friends. Imaginary friends. "Jesus loves me, this I know." Birthday parties. Holidays. Soccer. Flashcards. Candy Land. Colors. ABCs. Kindergarten. The Pledge of Allegiance. Phonics. Catching a ball. Throwing up. Reading their name. Drawing hearts. Dr. Seuss. Swimming. Addition. Geography. Bible verses. Computers. Plastic baseball bats. American Girl dolls. Opinions on clothes. Mud. Strangers. Questions about God. Subtraction. Homework. Signing report cards that could have been better. Friends moving away. Spelling. Goldfish, gerbil, guinea pig, dog, cat. Best friends. Hurt feelings. Multiplication tables. Long division. Baking. Tryouts. Piano lessons. Astronomy. Two-wheel bike. Questions about Jesus. Abstract thinking. Justice. Freedom. Worldview. Middle school. High school. Handing out $20 bills on demand. Driving. Dating. Bending curfew. College. Military. Work. Weddings. Phone call from the new dad. Grandparenting.

Lots of milestones. Lots of opportunities to mess up. Lots of opportunities to start fresh. You'll notice that each season seems to go faster and faster. And faster.

Still, each season brings the same assignment for moms and dads. *To know your kids.* Who are they? What do they need? How can I best meet those needs? As you move through each season, expect every family member to grow, learn, and change. Including you.

Through it all, remember to look for opportunities to celebrate and console. To give and receive. To serve and be served. To love and be loved. Give yourself permission to love abundantly. While also opening the door to your child's love. Show appreciation for who they are. No matter what.

Love without expecting anything in return. And you will get it all back, overflowing beyond measure.

TOPICAL INDEX

Note: Numbers are Strategy numbers
(not page numbers)

Note: Numbers are Strategy numbers
(not page numbers)

ACKNOWLEDGMENTS

Thanks to

My beloved bride, Rita, who is a millionfold better parent than I will ever be. Her inspiration can be found on every page.

My five mostly tolerable grown kids: Alec, Randall, Max, Isaac, and Rae Anne, who allowed me to practice parenting on them. You survived!

My six absolutely perfect grandchildren—all under four—who have given me fresh eyes for the privilege and joy of being part of a growing, loving family.

My cheerleaders and friends at the Steve Laube Agency, who steered this project over to Bethany House. Nicely done.

The astute editorial team: Andy McGuire, Jeff Braun, and Nancy Renich, who caught the vision, encouraged me, and polished the manuscript. Also, the shrewd marketing team, including Shawn Tabatt, Grace Kasper, and Chandler Smith, who is helping to spread the good news about this unique little resource.

Thanks especially to the untold number of moms and dads who continue to take my simple parenting ideas and deploy them to love on your own kids. Serving you is a privilege I do not take lightly.